# PRE-RAPHAELITES AND OLYMPIANS

......

Selected Works of Victorian Art
from the John and Julie Schaeffer and the
Art Gallery of New South Wales Collections

ART GALLERY NSW

This publication accompanies an exhibition of Victorian paintings and sculpture on display between 19 April and 9 September 2001 in the John and Julie Schaeffer Gallery at the Art Gallery of New South Wales, Sydney, Australia. It includes only those British works from the John and Julie Schaeffer and Art Gallery of New South Wales collections currently on display.



Published by the Art Gallery of New South Wales 2001


National Library of Australia
Cataloguing-in-publication data:
Beresford, Richard
Pre-Raphaelites & Olympians: selected works of Victorian Art from the John and Julie Schaeffer and the Art Gallery of New South Wales collections

Includes index.
ISBN 0-7347-6319-0

1. Schaeffer, John – Art collections – Exhibitions.
2. Schaeffer, Julie – Art collections – Exhibitions.
3. Art Gallery of New South Wales – Exhibitions.
4. Pre-Raphaelitism – England – Exhibitions.
5. Painting, Victorian – England – Exhibitions.
6. Sculpture, Victorian – England – Exhibitions.
9. Painting – Private collections — New South Wales – Sydney – Exhibitions.
10 Sculpture, British – Private collections – New South Wales – Sydney – Exhibitions. I. Art Gallery of New South Wales II. Title

Author: Richard Beresford
Designed by Graeme Walker
Photography by Jenni Carter, Brenton McGeachie, Lucio Nigro, and Ray Woodbury

Film by Spitting Image, Sydney
Printed by Pot Still Press, Sydney

Cover:
John Roddam Spencer Stanhope,
*Love and the Maiden* 1877 (detail)

# CONTENTS

......

5
FOREWORD

7
THE PRE-RAPHAELITE BROTHERHOOD:
some associates and contemporaries

15
ROSSETTI

21
BURNE-JONES AND HIS FOLLOWERS

28
WATTS

34
LEIGHTON

46
ALMA-TADEMA AND POYNTER

53
WATERHOUSE

56
LEIGHTON AND THE 'NEW SCULPTURE'

64
INDEX

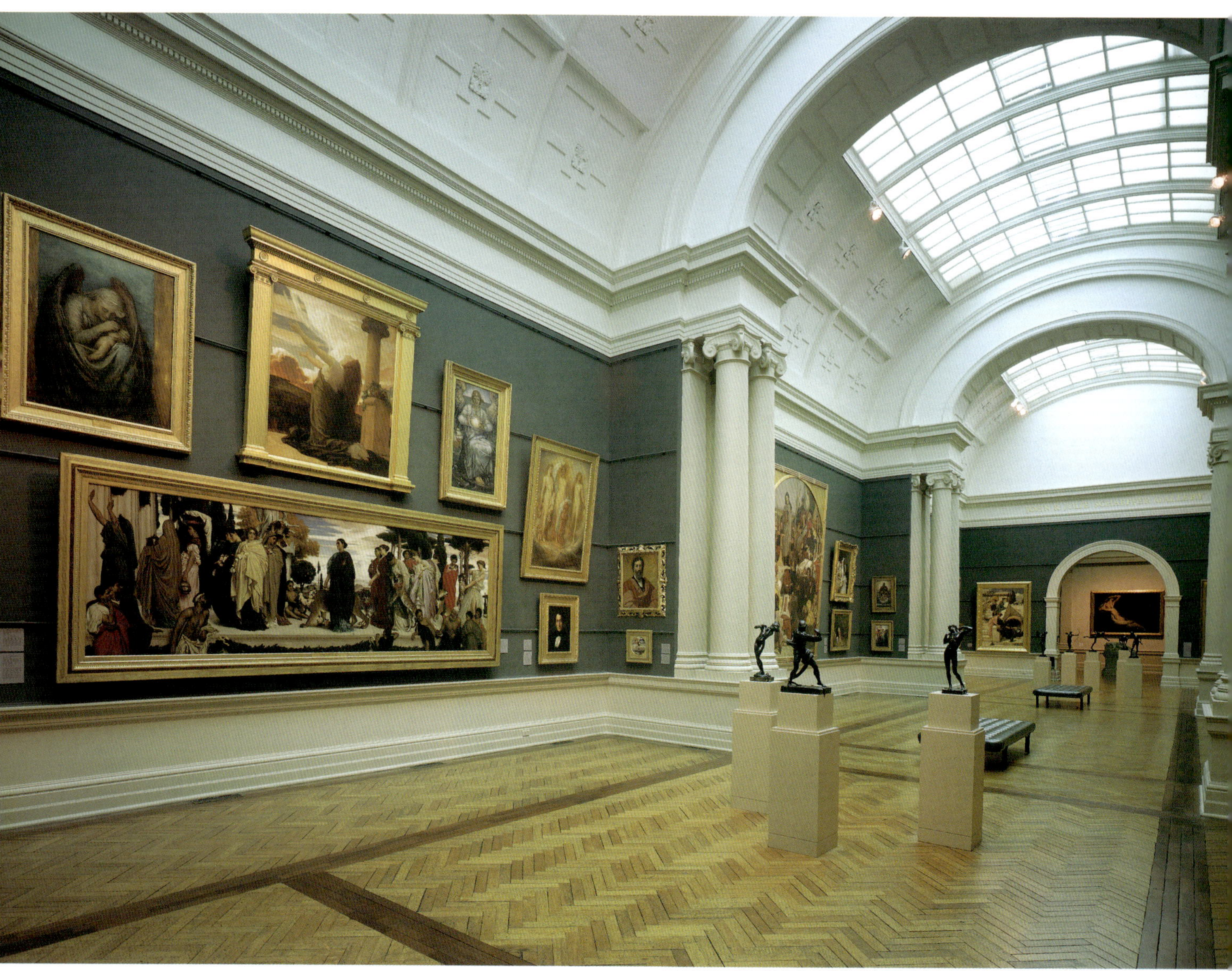

# FOREWORD

......

It is almost inconceivable that among the very first ten paintings acquired by this Gallery is Ford Madox Brown's epic and magisterial *Chaucer at the Court of Edward III*, bought directly from the artist in 1876. This is a most remarkable painting, not only for its scale but philosophically in its wholehearted embrace of the Pre-Raphaelite vision to rekindle a sense of profundity and a certain stylized aesthetic inspired by early Italian Renaissance art, and in the distinctly patriotic flavour of its subject. This great painting was joined in the Gallery before the end of the 19th century by similarly remarkable works including Leighton's *Wedded* (acquired 1882), Waterhouse's *Diogenes* (acquired 1886) and Poynter's masterful orchestration of the exotic *The Visit of the Queen of Sheba to King Solomon* purchased by the Gallery in 1892 just two years after its completion. Such acquisitions so early in the history of the Gallery laid the foundations for what is now an impressive and sizeable collection of British Victorian painting, one that vies with any outside England in its range and quality. It is a collection to which further works have been consistently if infrequently added. Among the acquisitions of recent decades are Leighton's sublime *Cymon and Iphigenia* (1976), Watts's *Artemis and Hyperion* (1983), various studies for Poynter's *Queen of Sheba* and Leighton's *Cymon and Iphigenia*, *Wedded* and *Winding the Skein* (in the 1980s and 90s) and, most recently, Alma Tadema's classic and beautiful *A Juggler* which was donated by John and Julie Schaeffer in 1999. Which, of course, brings us conveniently to the Schaeffers and their spectacular and passionate pursuit of great Victorian and 19th-century paintings and sculptures.

The emergence of the Schaeffer collection of Pre-Raphaelite, Victorian Olympian and 19th-century European paintings is very much a recent and living phenomenon driven by their personal love and fascination for these mysterious, intriguing, beautiful, at times melancholy but always romantic and poetic, pictures. It is most unusual that a private collection of such quality and imagination should so perfectly coincide with and complement that of a major art museum; but that is just the case with the Schaeffer and the Art Gallery of New South Wales collections. The combined resources of these two collections of Victorian and related paintings has resulted in a more coherent, substantive and comprehensive display of such works than anything which even the most ambitious of our forbears could have dreamed of. This publication celebrates an outstanding moment in the history of the Gallery. For the first time we can write the story of Victorian art drawing almost exclusively on Sydney collections. The story is not, of course, quite complete, and could never be, even in the context of a major international exhibition. Nevertheless it is an infinitely richer, deeper and more intriguing one than anything we could have hoped to tell without the very extensive and generous loans from the Schaeffers. We are also grateful to the Trustees of the National Gallery of Victoria who have kindly agreed to augment our representation of Rossetti and Alma Tadema by the loan of major works from their collection. Above all we extend our deepest thanks to John and Julie Schaeffer and trust that they will derive as much pleasure as our visitors in seeing the gallery which now bears their names, so richly furnished with our joint collections of Pre-Raphaelite and Olympian paintings.

Edmund Capon,
Director

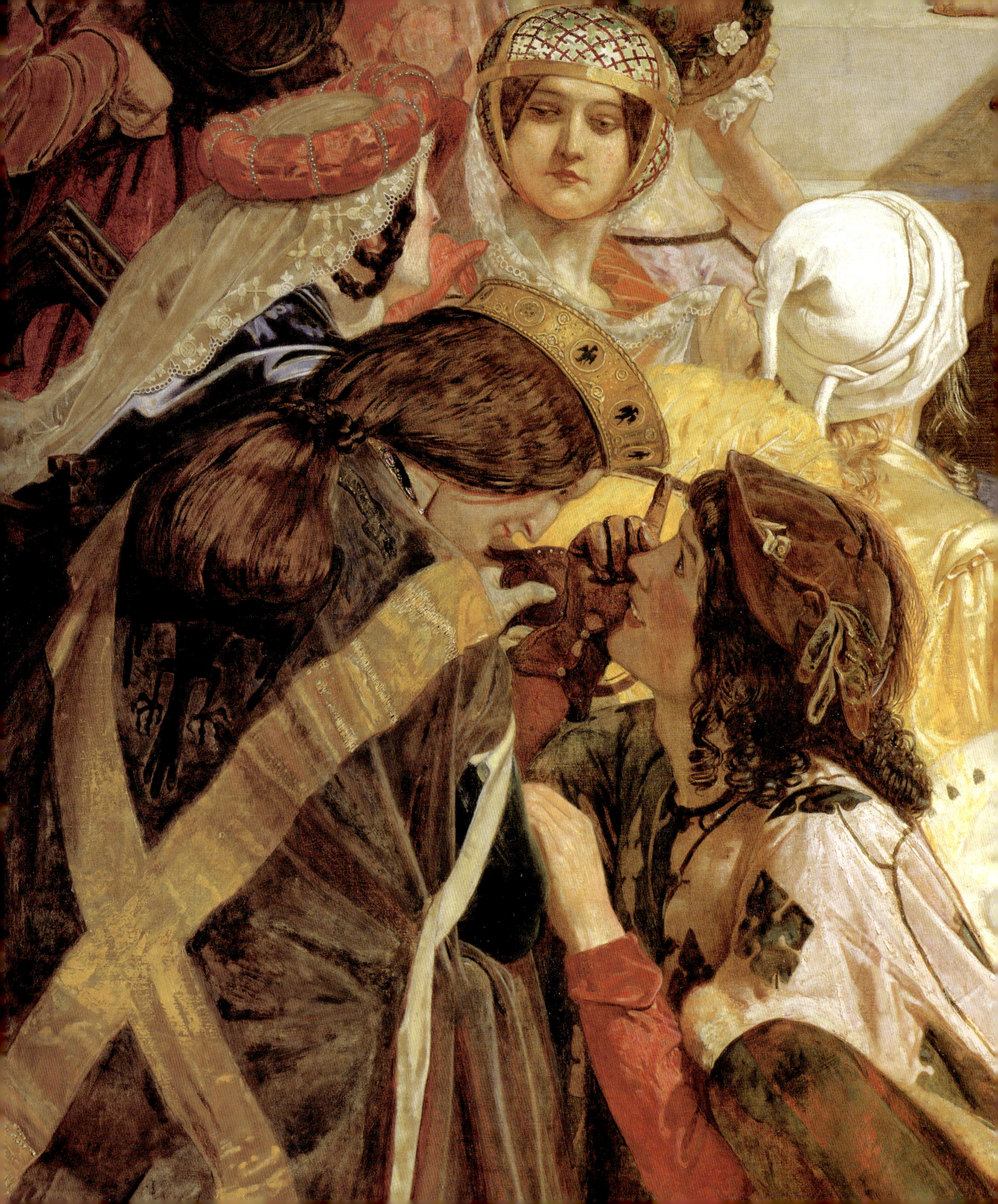

# THE PRE-RAPHAELITE BROTHERHOOD: some Associates and Contemporaries

……

The Pre-Raphaelite Brotherhood was formed in the autumn of 1848. Essentially it was an association of three talented young art students (one of whom was still in his teens, the others scarcely older) who wished to challenge the traditional teachings of the Royal Academy. The artists in question were Dante Gabriel Rossetti, William Holman Hunt and John Everett Millais. During the years which followed the formation of the brotherhood they exhibited a succession of revolutionary works which turned to the example of the early-Italian school (those artists who worked before Raphael) to inject a new earnestness and sincerity into British painting. The essential tenets of the brotherhood were that their works should treat serious subjects and that they should do so with unswerving fidelity to nature.

The story of the Pre-Raphaelite Brotherhood in its early years is well-known and cannot be retold through the works in Sydney collections. The paintings which were exhibited with the provocatively mysterious initials 'PRB' and the further major early works of Rossetti, Hunt and Millais have to be studied in British public collections. On the other hand there is in Sydney a painting which sits conspicuously on the sidelines of this story. Ford Madox Brown has been described as the 'founder of Pre-Raphaelitism' and, as we know from a letter to Holman Hunt, he entertained the idea of inscribing the PRB initials on the most ambitious canvas of his career, his *Chaucer at the Court of Edward III.*

Brown's relationship to the brotherhood and to the impact which it made on British art is in fact rather difficult to define. He was a somewhat older artist and one of much wider experience. He had been trained in Belgium and was familiar with the contemporary art scene in Paris. When he started work on *Chaucer*, he was living in Rome where he came into contact with that earnest group of German artists, the Nazarenes, who were engaged in an attempt to revitalise contemporary religious painting by reference to early-Italian models. It was to Brown that Rossetti turned for tuition in 1848, immediately prior to the formation of the brotherhood, and it was thus in a studio dominated by the unfinished *Chaucer* that he first established a lifelong rapport with the older artist. Rossetti was without doubt the intellectual leader of the Pre-Raphaelite brotherhood, but the influence of Brown on his thinking was probably greater than is generally acknowledged. At the same time, it was the converse influence of the Pre-Raphaelite brothers on Brown which caused him, as he worked on the *Chaucer*, to turn it more and more into a Pre-Raphaelite picture.

The Pre-Raphaelite 'brotherhood' was not long-lived. With Millais's election as an Associate of the Royal Academy in 1853 and Hunt's departure for the Middle East in the following year it had essentially ceased to exist. Yet there remained a certain coherence in the productions of the brothers and those influenced by them which permits a 'first phase' of Pre-Raphaelitism to be distinguished, which lasted until c.1860. Thereafter the paths of the Pre-Raphaelite brothers diverged. Rossetti's work of the 1860s and 1870s, which we can claim with hindsight was the most significant for the later development of British art, is the subject of the following section. Here we bring together works by Hunt and Millais along with a number of others which in varying degrees and in varying ways have some association with the early story of Pre-Raphaelitism.

• **Ford Madox Brown** *Chaucer at the Court of Edward III* 1847-51 (detail)

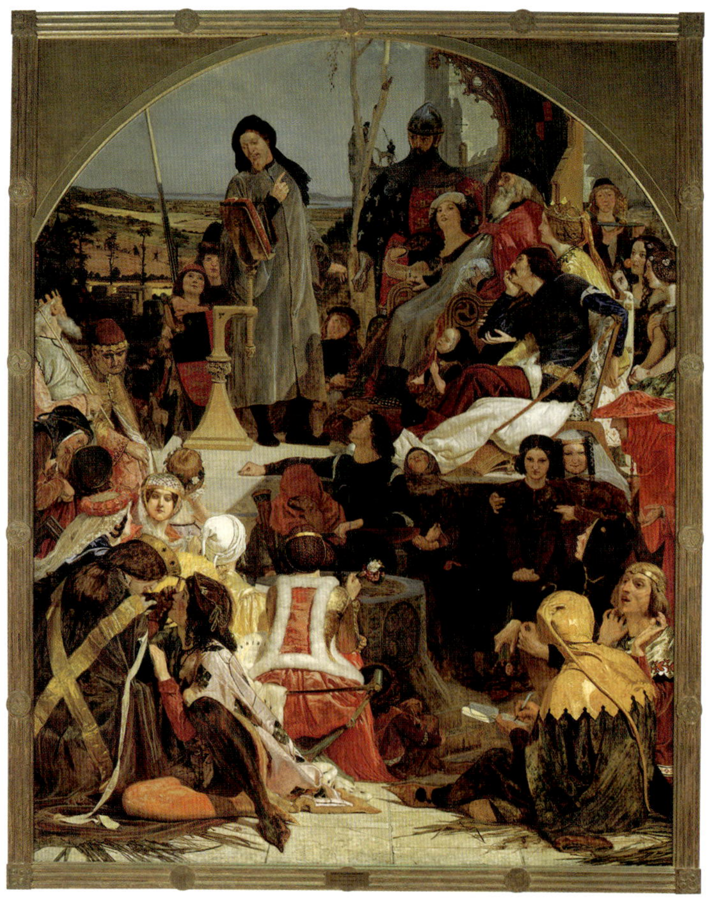

FORD MADOX BROWN (1821-1893)
*Chaucer at the Court of Edward III* 1847-51
oil on canvas, the spandrels gilt 372 x 296 cm
Art Gallery of New South Wales, purchased 1876

The scale of this work and its patriotic subject matter were almost certainly inspired by the artist's desire to obtain one of the commissions for murals in the new London Houses of Parliament. It was probably with this prospect in mind that Brown moved from Paris to London in 1844. In Mackintosh's *History of England* he chanced on a reference which immediately inspired in him, as he later recalled, 'visions of Chaucer reading his poems to knights & Ladyes fair, to king & court amid air & sunshine'. Such a subject would celebrate 'the origins of our native tongue'. Initial work on the design was undertaken in Rome and the present canvas was begun in London in 1847. Over the four years which it took him to complete it, Brown became a close associate of Rossetti and the Pre-Raphaelite Brotherhood. He witnessed the vilification of their early exhibits by the press and in 1851, the year in which *Chaucer* was exhibited, the influential defence of Ruskin. Brown's essential aim was to depict a significant historical event just as it might have appeared. The project was pursued with close attention to historical accuracy and under Pre-Raphaelite influence with increasing concern for truth to nature, especially with regard to the effect of muted English summer sunshine. Brown also began to use his friends rather than professionals for models, appropriately asking the poet-painter Rossetti to sit for Chaucer.

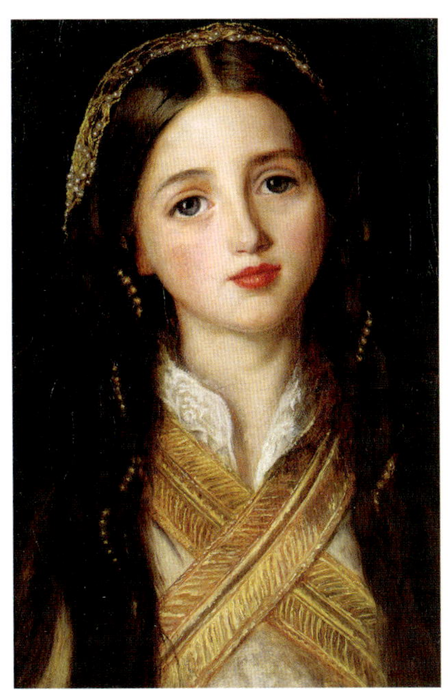

SIR JOHN EVERETT MILLAIS (1829-1896)
*Alice Gray* 1857
oil on canvas 30.5 x 20.3 cm
John and Julie Schaeffer Collection

Millais was the most naturally talented of the Pre-Raphaelite brothers. In 1853 he began work on a portrait of John Ruskin and fell in love with Ruskin's wife Effie. The annulment of the Ruskin marriage and Millais's subsequent marriage to Effie caused a great public scandal in 1855. The present picture is one of a pair of portraits of the painter's new sisters-in-law, Alice and Sophie Gray, painted in 1857. The sisters also modelled for *Autumn Leaves* (Manchester City Art Gallery) one of the most celebrated works of Millais's Pre-Raphaelite period. By 1860 Millais had abandoned Pre-Raphaelite principles to pursue a more conventional (and hugely successful) career.

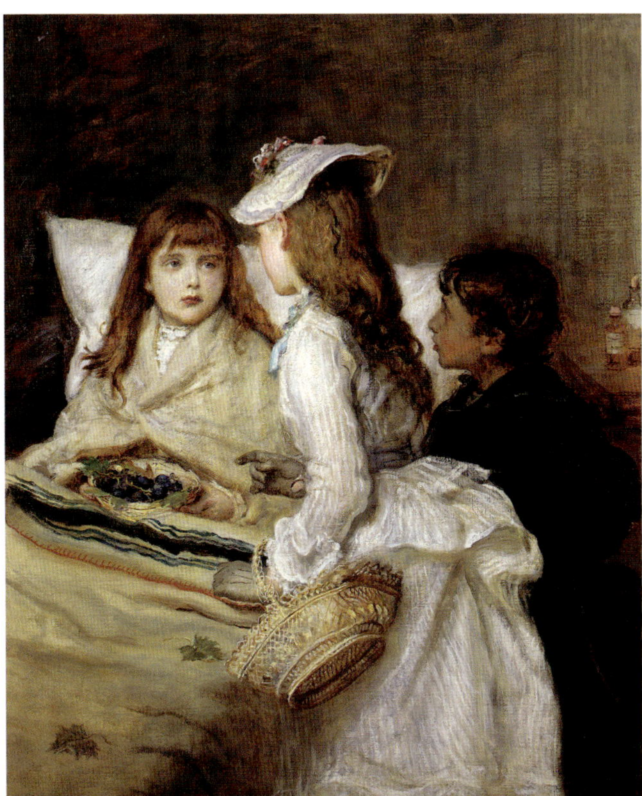

SIR JOHN EVERETT MILLAIS
*Getting Better* 1876
oil on canvas 103 x 91 cm
John and Julie Schaeffer Collection

The picture began life as part of another painting, Millais's *North-West Passage* of 1874 in the Tate Gallery, which was originally to have two children in the upper right-hand corner turning a globe. When he decided to simplify the composition Millais cut away this section of canvas and later used the blocked out figures as the basis for the present picture. The model for the convalescent girl is not certain (it may have been one of the artist's nieces), but for her visitors Millais used his own children, the fourteen-year-old Alice for the girl, and the eleven-year-old John Guille for the boy. The latter was to become his father's biographer.

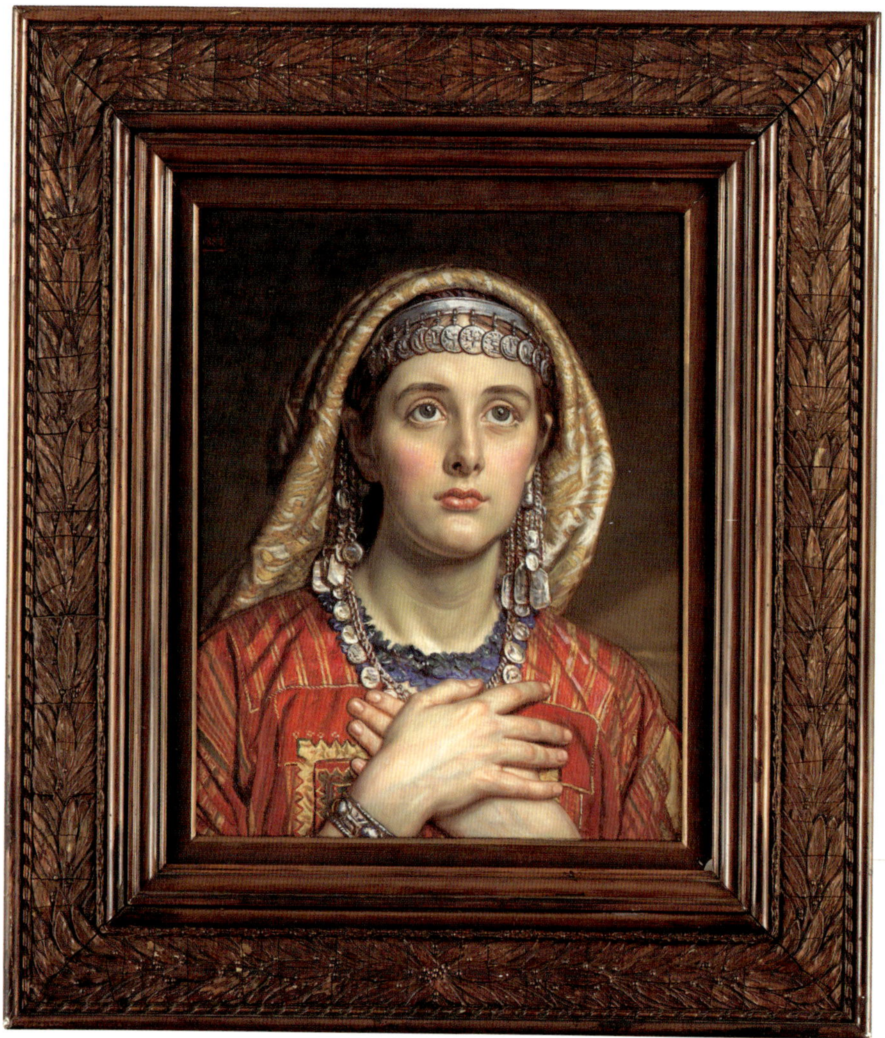

WILLIAM HOLMAN HUNT (1827-1910)
*The Bride of Bethlehem* 1884
oil over tempera on canvas 50.8 x 41.3 cm
John and Julie Schaeffer Collection

Holman Hunt was the only one of the Pre-Raphaelites who remained faithful to the principles of the brotherhood throughout his life. During the painting of his *Light of the World*, the most famous religious image of the Victorian era, he experienced a conversion and much of his later work treated biblical themes. It was entirely characteristic of the artist that in order to paint such subjects with the utmost fidelity he made a number of trips to the Bible lands. The present picture seems to have served as a study for the head of the Virgin Mary in one of the artist's most ambitious late works, the *Triumph of the Innocents*, a painting begun in Jerusalem in 1875 and completed only after a long struggle in 1887 (Walker Art Gallery, Liverpool).

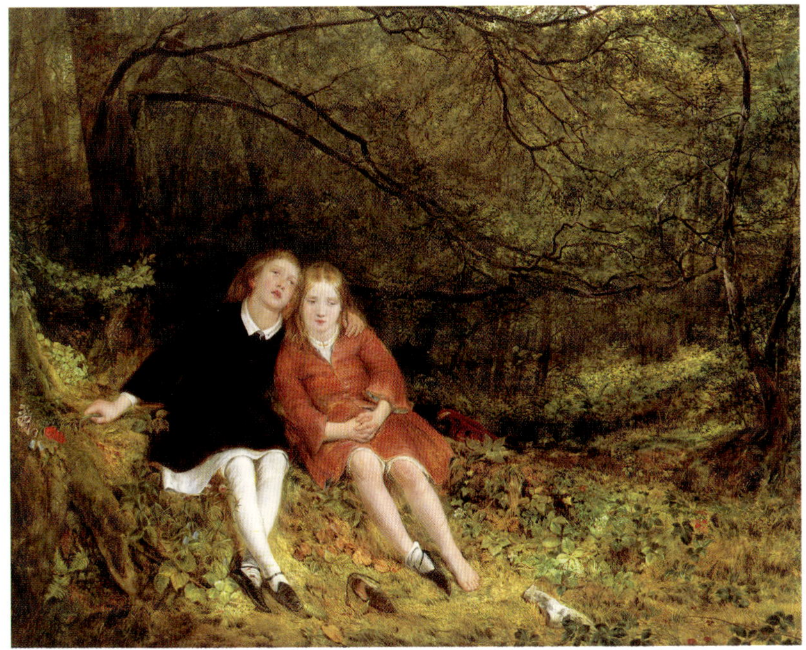

RICHARD REDGRAVE (1804-1888)
*The Lost Path* 1852
oil on canvas 77.5 x 101.6 cm
John and Julie Schaeffer Collection

When exhibited at the Royal Academy exhibition of 1853 this picture attracted highly favourable comment. Redgrave's woodland scenes were admired for their minute handling which was regarded by critics as 'Pre-Raphaelite'. Indeed the artist may well have been inspired by Millais's *Ophelia* which was exhibited in the same year that this picture was painted. Redgrave was also involved with running the Schools of Design and worked as Surveyor of the Queen's Pictures in which capacity he produced a manuscript catalogue of the Royal Collection. With his brother Samuel he also wrote an important history of British painting, *A Century of Painters of the British School*, which appeared in 1866.

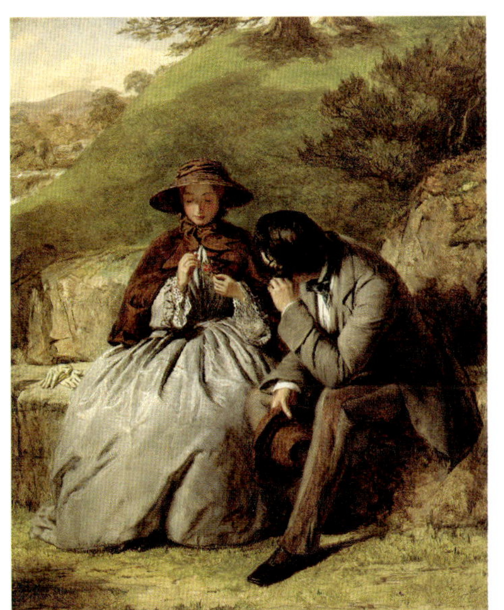

WILLIAM POWELL FRITH (1819-1909)
*Lovers* 1855
oil on board 36 x 30 cm
John and Julie Schaeffer Collection

Frith started his career as a painter of historical and literary subjects, but in the 1850s was encouraged by the success of the Pre-Raphaelites to turn his hand to subjects from modern life. In 1854 his *Ramsgate Sands*, a panoramic view of Victorian beach life, was a huge success at the Royal Academy and was purchased by Queen Victoria. The more modest *Lovers*, exhibited in the following year, takes a time-honoured romantic subject and places it firmly within the sphere of contemporary life.

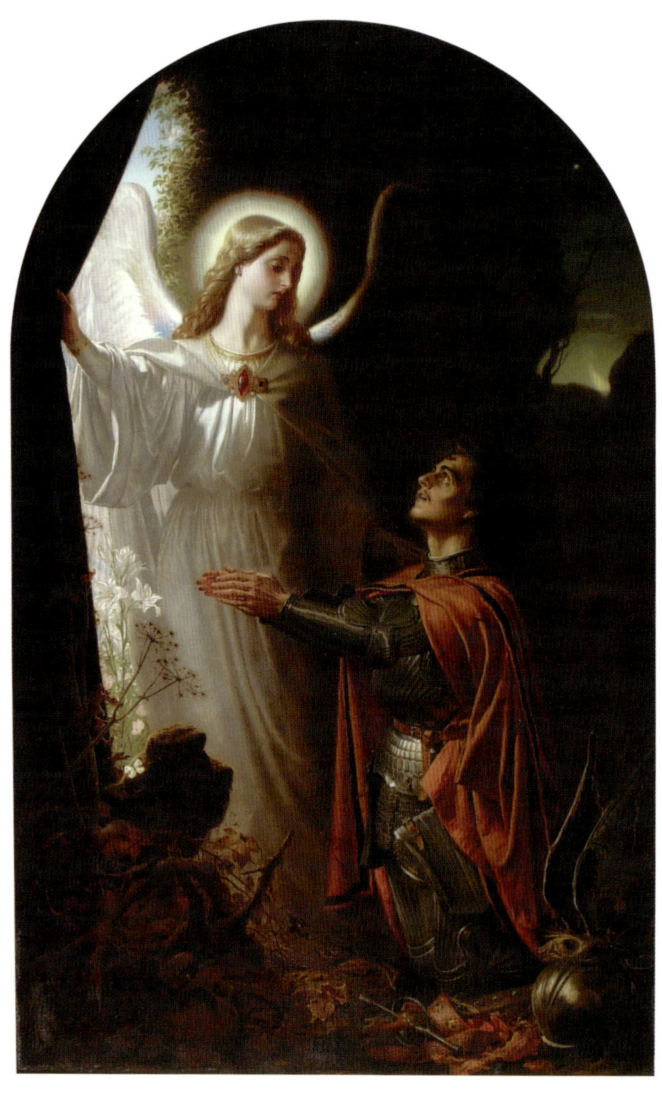

SIR JOSEPH NOEL PATON (1821-1901)
*Mors Janua Vitae (The Gate of Life)* 1866
oil on canvas 116.9 x 73.7 cm
John and Julie Schaeffer Collection

Paton was a Scottish artist with strong leanings toward Pre-Raphaelitism. During a period in London in the 1840s he met Millais with whom he became lifelong friends. The present picture is the first in the sequence of paintings with religious themes which were to dominate the artist's production after c.1870. The subject is explained in the catalogue of the Royal Academy exhibition of 1866. It shows a knight on the threshold of death: 'And the Shadow spake, and its voice was as the voice of an angel: "Thou hast been faithful unto death; and the Lord will give thee a crown of Life"'. The meticulously observed suit of armour is based on one in the artist's own collection.

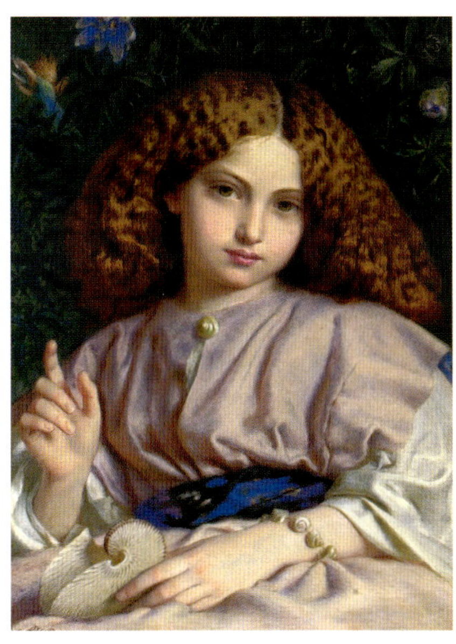

SIR FREDERIC WILLIAM BURTON (1816-1900)
*The Child Miranda* 1864
watercolour with gum arabic and bodycolour over pencil on paper 37.5 x 27.3 cm
John and Julie Schaeffer Collection

Burton was an Irish watercolour painter, chiefly known for his subject pictures which often dealt with themes from Irish life. This child portrait, however, with the prominence of shells and the fairy discretely introduced among the backdrop of passion-flowers, has a mysterious air of ungraspable significance – a presage Symbolism. In 1874 Burton gave up painting to become Director of the National Gallery in London, a position which he held for twenty years.

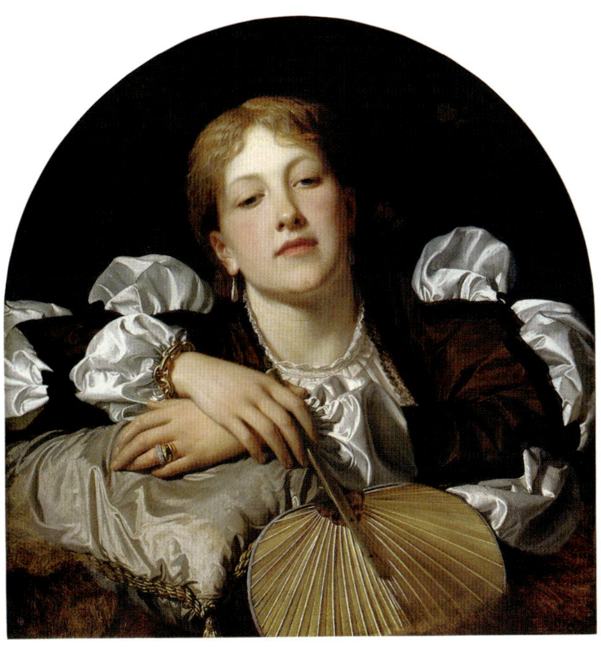

CHARLES EDWARD PERUGINI (1839-1918)
*"I know a maiden fair to see, take care"* 1868
oil on paper laid down on canvas 55.9 x 55.9 cm
John and Julie Schaeffer Collection

The picture was exhibited at the Royal Academy in 1868 and was acquired by Millais. The title is a quotation from Longfellow's translation of a German poem which appeared in his *Poems and Poetry of Europe* in 1843: 'I know a maiden fair to see / Take care! / She can both false and friendly be, / Beware! Beware! / Trust her not / She is fooling thee'. The Italian-born artist arrived in London in 1863 and married Charles Dickens's daughter Kate, who also became a painter, as well as sitting on occasion for Millais. He later became a protégé of Leighton and painted some fine classical works.

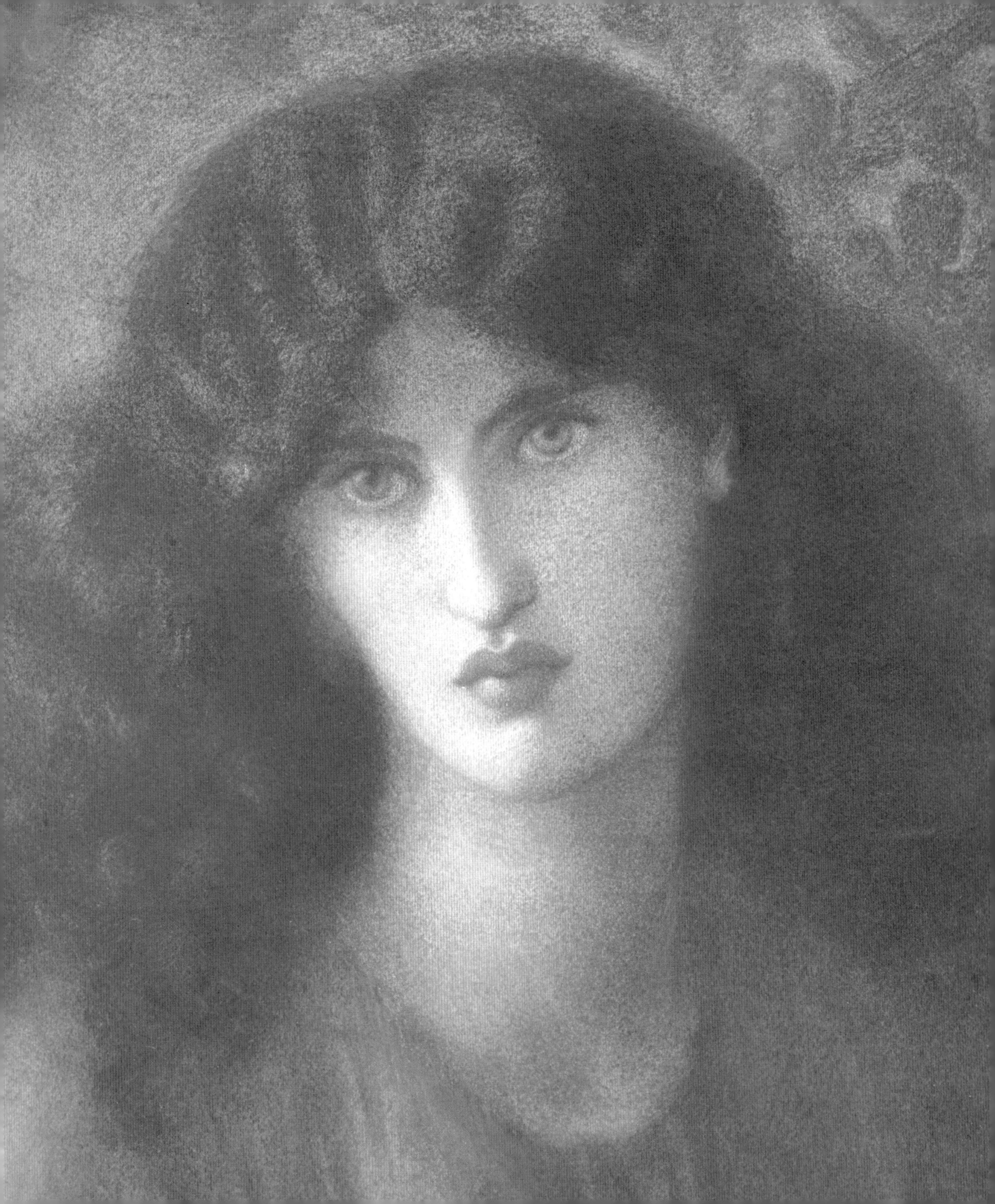

# ROSSETTI

......

If Rossetti was the leading intellectual force behind the Pre-Raphaelite brotherhood, his public career as a Pre-Raphaelite painter was brief. He was the first of the group to exhibit an overtly Pre-Raphaelite work, showing his *Girlhood of the Virgin Mary* at the Free Exhibition in 1849 (Tate Gallery). However, in the following year his *Ecce Ancilla Domini* (also Tate Gallery) was bitterly attacked by the critics and he vowed never to exhibit in public again. He also largely abandoned oil painting and instead during the 1850s produced mainly drawings and intricately worked watercolours on medievalising themes, the subjects frequently drawn from the poetry of Dante.

Thus by the age of twenty-three Rossetti had essentially decided to retire from the public arena. From around this time we can trace the first of his obsessive love affairs with beautiful women, which would become the focus of his life, as of his art. The first was Elizabeth Siddal who by 1852 was living with Rossetti in Chatham Place near Blackfriars Bridge. The artist was obsessed with her beauty, which was clearly remarkable (Ruskin described her as 'beautiful as the reflection of a golden mountain in a crystal lake'). In 1860 he finally married her, but by this time her health was already in decline and their relationship was becoming more strained. Two years into their marriage Lizzie (or 'Guggums' as Rossetti called her) took an overdose of laudanum from which she died. Whether this was suicide is not certain.

The remainder of Rossetti's life reads like the synopsis of an opera. An impassioned quest for art and beauty takes place in a colourful setting of eccentric bohemianism; youthful merriment gives way to obsessive passion, tragedy, despair and death. After Lizzie Siddal's death Rossetti moved to the large, if somewhat dilapidated, Queen Anne House in Cheyne Walk which was to become the setting for the artist's famously reclusive and eccentric lifestyle. In the house he accumulated a burgeoning collection of antique furniture and china, which is not so surprising as a menagerie of exotic pets which included a raccoon, armadillos, wallabies and a wombat. It was in this bizarre context that Rossetti's art evolved in the 1860s into something quite individual. He mastered the technique of oil painting and, working now on a larger scale, devoted himself to the depiction of voluptuous female beauty.

A notoriously macabre episode took place in 1869, when Rossetti obtained permission to exhume the remains of Lizzie Siddal in order to recover the manuscript of his early poetry which he had buried with her. With some additions the collection was published in 1870 under the title *Poems*. The volume sold well, but was the subject of a bitter attack by Robert Buchanan in his pamphlet *The Fleshly School of Poetry* which appeared in 1871. Rossetti's extreme sensitivity to criticism had already been manifest, but it now developed into paranoia. He became yet more reclusive receiving only a small circle of friends. At the same time he suffered from acute insomnia for which he took large doses of the drug chloral which, along with alcohol, ultimately undermined his health. Rossetti's work was not known to a wide public until after his death in 1882 and he had few close followers. Nevertheless his ideas and personality were a potent force in the later developments of Victorian painting toward Aestheticism and Symbolism.

• **Dante Gabriel Rossetti** *Pandora* 1869 (detail)

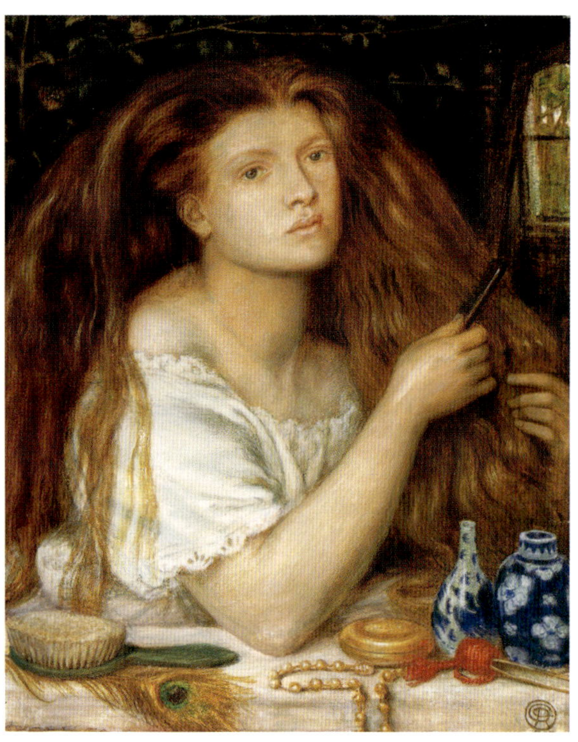

DANTE GABRIEL ROSSETTI (1828-1882)
*Woman combing her Hair* 1865
watercolour with gum arabic over pencil on paper laid on panel
44.5 x 37.5 cm
John and Julie Schaeffer Collection

From the 1860s Rossetti focussed almost exclusively on painting single female figures of characteristic voluptuousness. Many of these were without specific subject and he painted a number of variations on the theme of a woman at her toilet, often using as model his housekeeper and now mistress, Fanny Cornforth. In this case the sitter remains unidentified. Rossetti was an enthusiastic collector of blue and white porcelain such as that depicted on the toilet table.

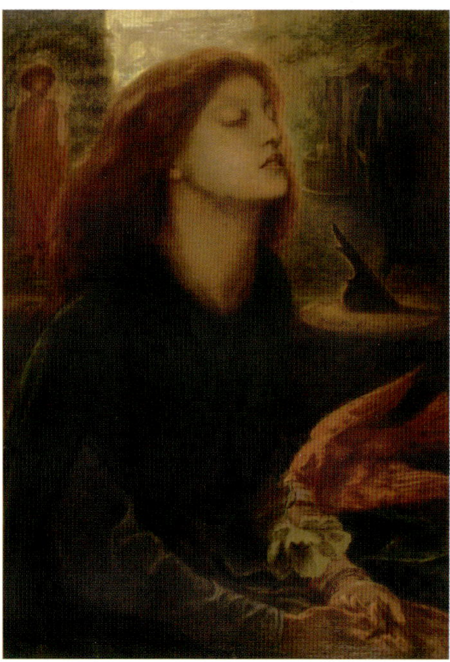

AFTER DANTE GABRIEL ROSSETTI
*Beata Beatrix*, the original 1864-70
oil on canvas 72 x 52 cm
John and Julie Schaeffer Collection

This is a faithful copy of one of Rossetti's most celebrated and moving works. At an uncertain date he had begun and abandoned a picture of Dante's lover Beatrice asleep. Lizzie Siddal was the model. In 1864, about two years after his wife's death, he returned to the canvas reworking it into a scene from Dante's *Vita Nuova*. It shows Beatrice sitting on her balcony overlooking Florence as she falls into a trance and is transported from earth to heaven. In the background are the figures of Love and Dante and a view of Florence. A red dove drops a poppy into Beatrice's hands symbolizing her death. The picture is at once Rossetti's last likeness of Lizzie Siddal ('one might almost say she sat in spirit' as his brother remarked) and a memorial to her.

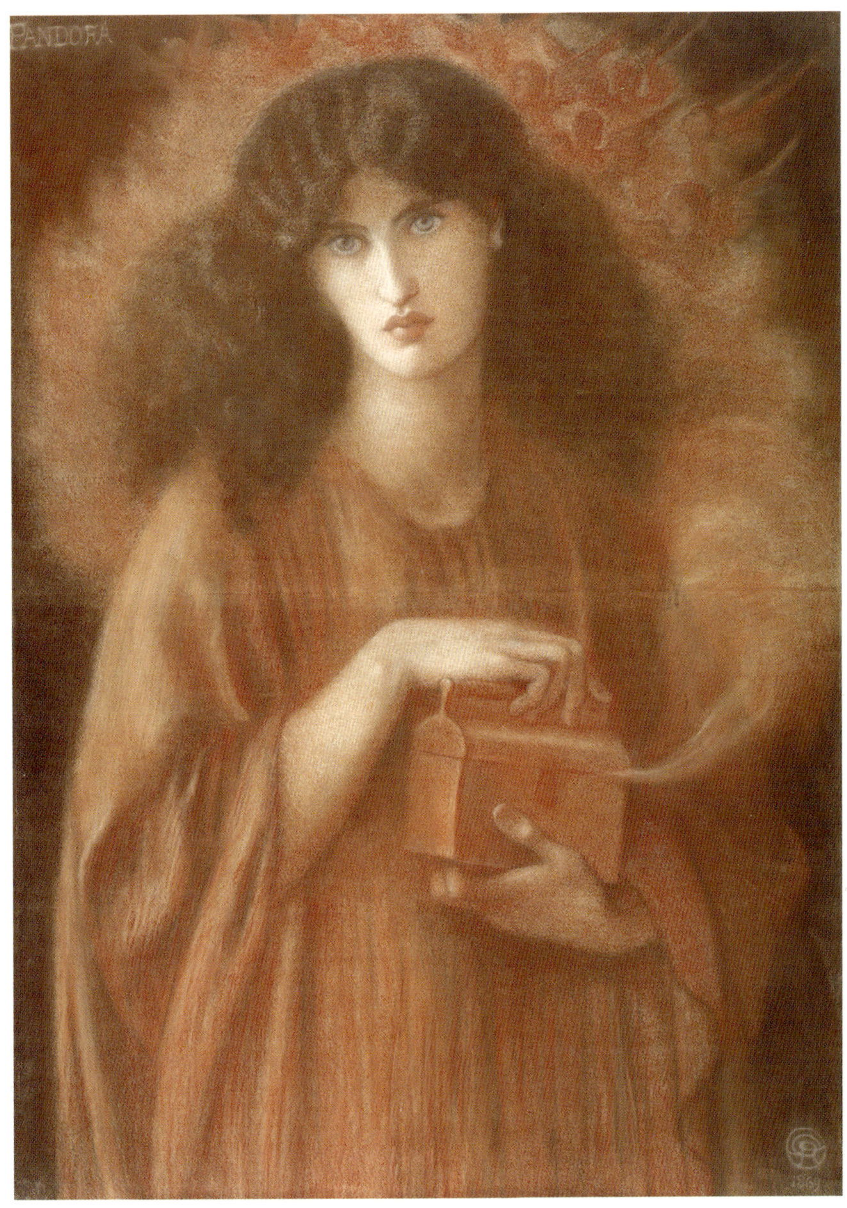


DANTE GABRIEL ROSSETTI
*Pandora* 1869
pastel on paper 94 x 66 cm
John and Julie Schaeffer Collection

Pandora opens the casket from which spill out all the ills destined to beset Mankind. It was by this means that Zeus revenged himself on the human race for Prometheus's theft of fire from heaven. The opening of the casket marks the end of the Golden Age. The choice of subject reflects Rossetti's obsession with the theme of the *femme fatale*. This pastel is one of two finished studies for an oil painting executed in 1871. The model was Jane Morris.

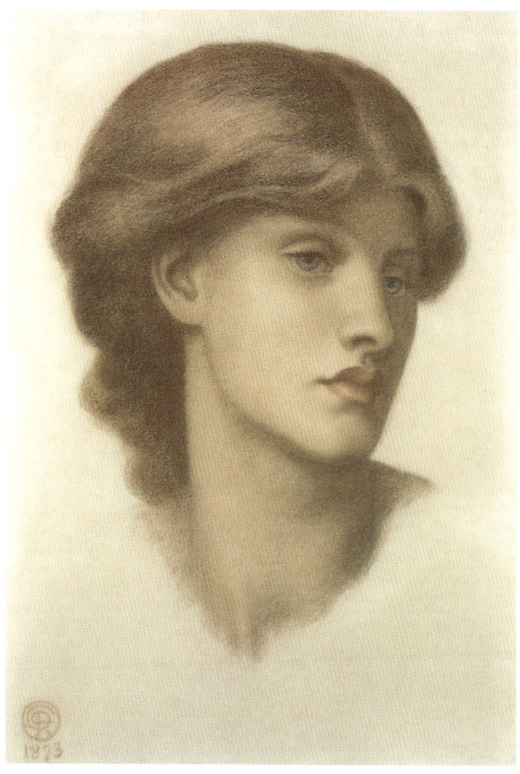

DANTE GABRIEL ROSSETTI
*Alexa Wilding* 1873
pastel on paper 53.3 x 38 cm
John and Julie Schaeffer Collection

The sitter for this head study was Alexa Wilding, one of Rossetti's favourite models of the 1860s and 1870s. His studio assistant Henry Treffry Dunn described her face as 'beautifully moulded in every feature, full of quiescent, soft, mystical repose that suited some of his conceptions admirably, but without any variety of expression. She sat like a Sphinx waiting to be questioned and with always a vague reply in return …'. She was the model for some of Rossetti's most important works.

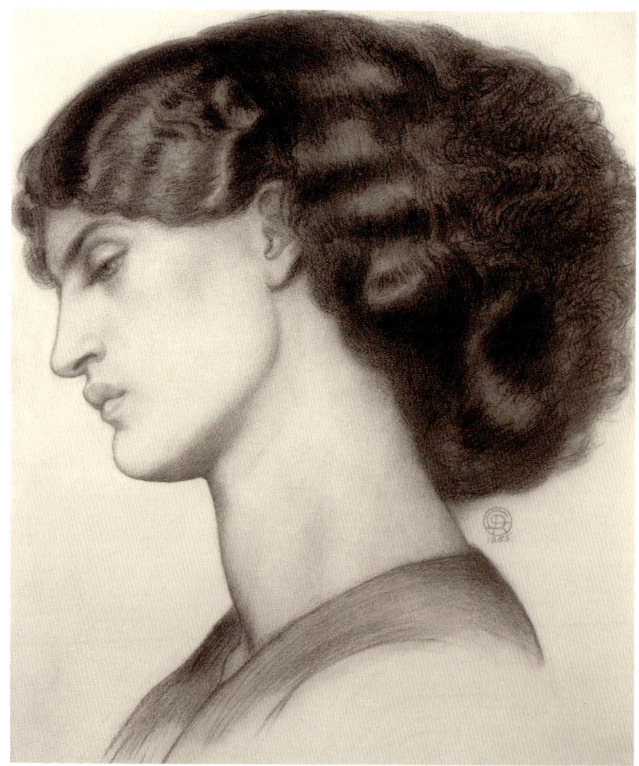

DANTE GABRIEL ROSSETTI
*Mrs William Morris* 1865
black chalk on paper 31.5 x 34.5 cm
John and Julie Schaeffer Collection

Rossetti first met the sitter, Jane Burden, in 1857 when he was working on the decoration of the Debating Chamber of the Oxford Union. William Morris who was working on the same project fell in love with her and they were married in 1859. Rossetti, however, remained deeply attracted to her and in the later 1860s they developed a close friendship. Jane Morris served as model for a number of Rossetti's works at this period, including *Pandora* (see p.17).

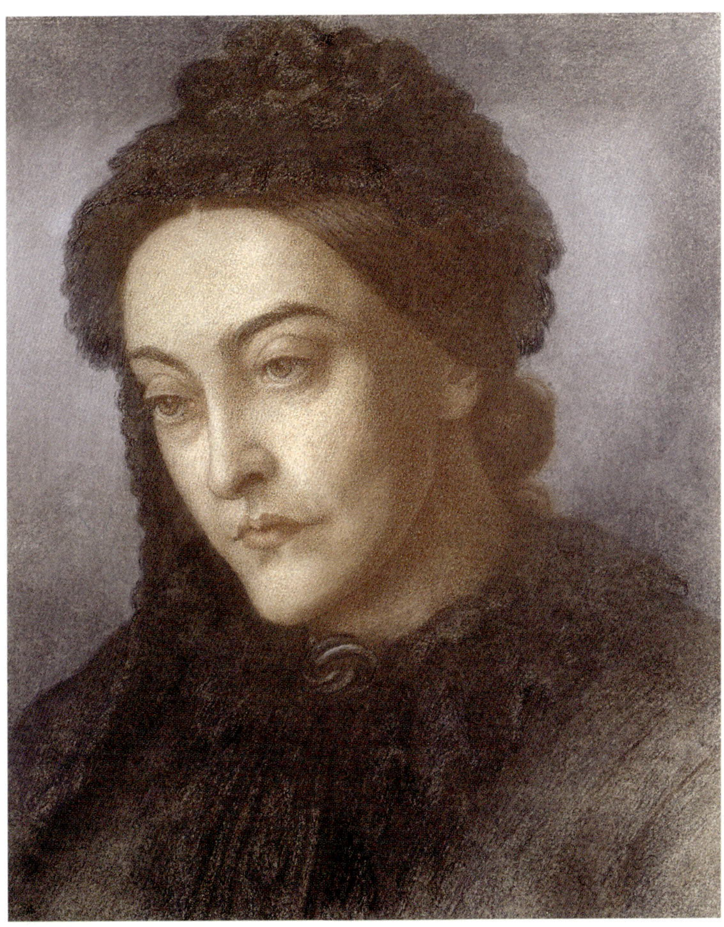

DANTE GABRIEL ROSSETTI
*Christina Rossetti* 1877
pastel on paper 43.2 x 35.6 cm
John and Julie Schaeffer Collection

During the summer of 1877, overcome with depression and the effects of the drug chloral, Rossetti suffered a breakdown. On his doctor's instructions he left London and settled in a country cottage at Hunter's Forestall on the north Kent coast. Over the next months he was tended by his nurse, mother and sister. At first a violent trembling of his hand induced a fear that he would never again be able to work. But by October he had sufficiently recovered to make a series of drawings of his mother and sister. The present pastel of Christina is the last of the group. It was described by F.G. Stephens as 'the best portrait of our poet-painter's devoted and constant sister, his refuge in dark and painful days'.

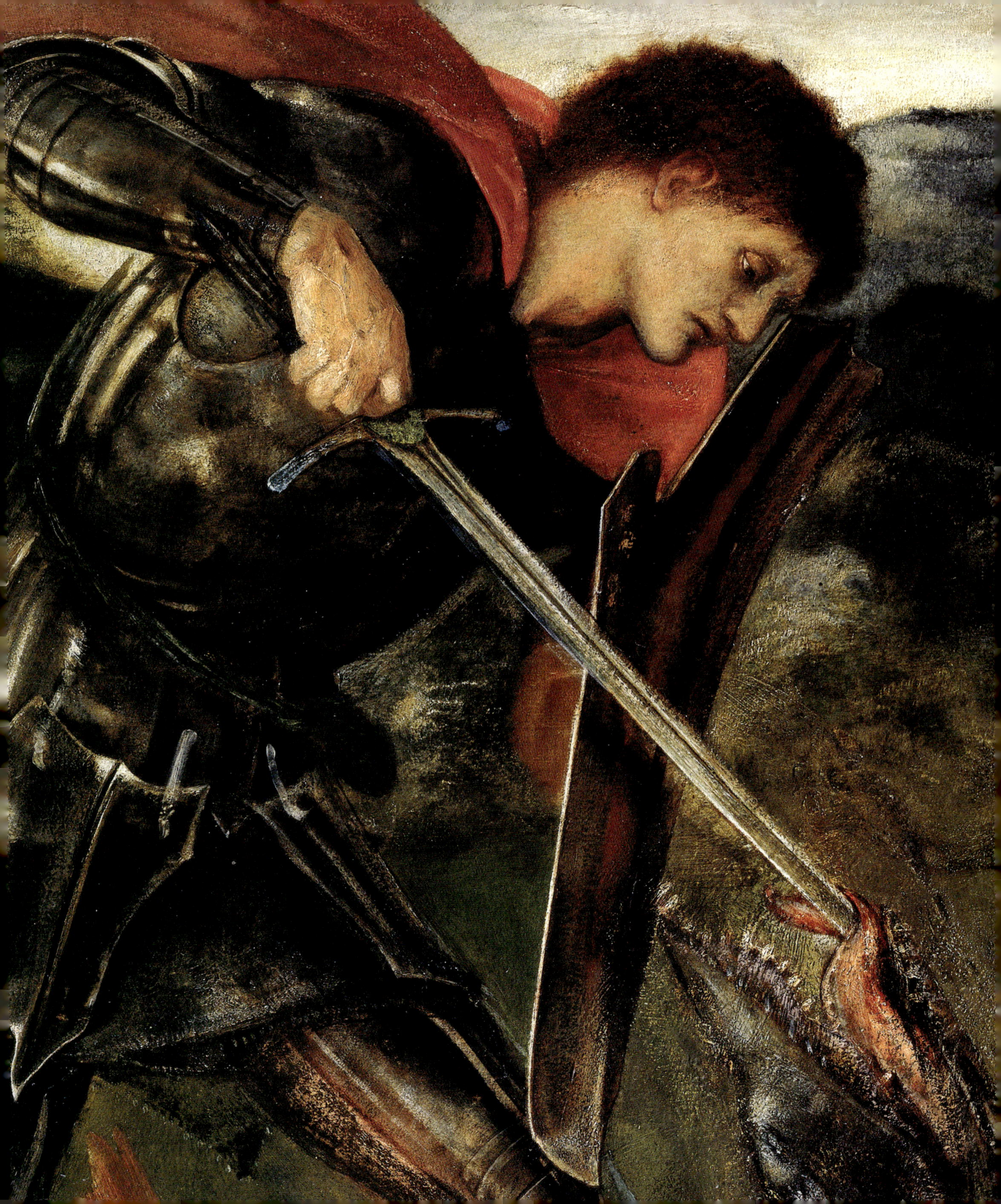

# BURNE-JONES AND HIS FOLLOWERS

......

Burne-Jones was the leading figure in the later evolution of Pre-Raphaelitism and, with his lifelong friend, William Morris was the artist chiefly responsible for expanding the new aesthetic into the decorative arts. He first met Morris as a fellow student at Exeter College, Oxford, at which time both men intended to go into the church. Under Ruskin's influence, however, and through him becoming familiar with the works of the Pre-Raphaelites, they determined to devote themselves to art.

Burne-Jones never received a formal artistic training and the principal influence on his work in the later 1850s was Rossetti from whom he took informal lessons. With Morris he was one of the group of artists brought together by Rossetti in 1857 to decorate the debating chamber of the Oxford Union with murals depicting scenes from Malory's *Morte d'Arthur*. In the later 1850s he received encouragement from both Watts and Ruskin and was persuaded to make study trips to Italy in 1859 and 1860. The artists of the Venetian school, especially Titian, impressed him deeply at this period and inspired a strong Venetian tendency in his work.

Burne-Jones had already distinguished himself as a designer of stained glass in the late 1850s and in 1861 he helped William Morris form the company of Morris, Marshall, Faulkner & Co for which he worked extensively, producing designs for stained glass and decorative arts. In 1864 he became an Associate of the Old Water-Colour Society and exhibited with the Society in the later 1860s. His work, however, was not always well-received and in reaction to complaints about the nudity of one of the figures in his *Phyllis and Demophoön* (Birmingham City Art Gallery) he resigned from the Society in 1870 and stopped exhibiting in public.

At this time his relations with Ruskin, Rossetti and Morris became more distant and he turned for inspiration to the works of the Italian Renaissance making two further trips to Italy in 1871 and 1873. In the mid-1870s Burne-Jones evolved his mature style, brilliantly represented for example in works such as the *Beguiling of Merlin* (Lady Lever Art Gallery, Port Sunlight). Then in 1877 he return with spectacular effect to the public arena, showing eight major works at the inaugural exhibition of the Grosvenor Gallery. These caused a sensation and immediately secured Burne-Jones's reputation as the leading artist of the Aesthetic movement.

Burne-Jones's later career was hugely successful and his influence was widely felt. Among the artists who exhibited with him at the Grosvenor Gallery in 1877 was John Roddam Spencer Stanhope. An artist of aristocratic origin, Stanhope had been living since 1873 in the Villa Nuti at Bellosguardo outside Florence. There he became absorbed with the works of the early Italian Renaissance, particularly those of Botticelli. One of his major exhibits in 1877 was the Schaeffer collection *Love and the Maiden*. Somewhat younger artists who may appropriately be considered in this context are John Dickson Batten and Edward Reginald Frampton.

• **Sir Edward Coley Burne-Jones** *The Fight: Saint George kills the Dragon VI* 1866 (detail)

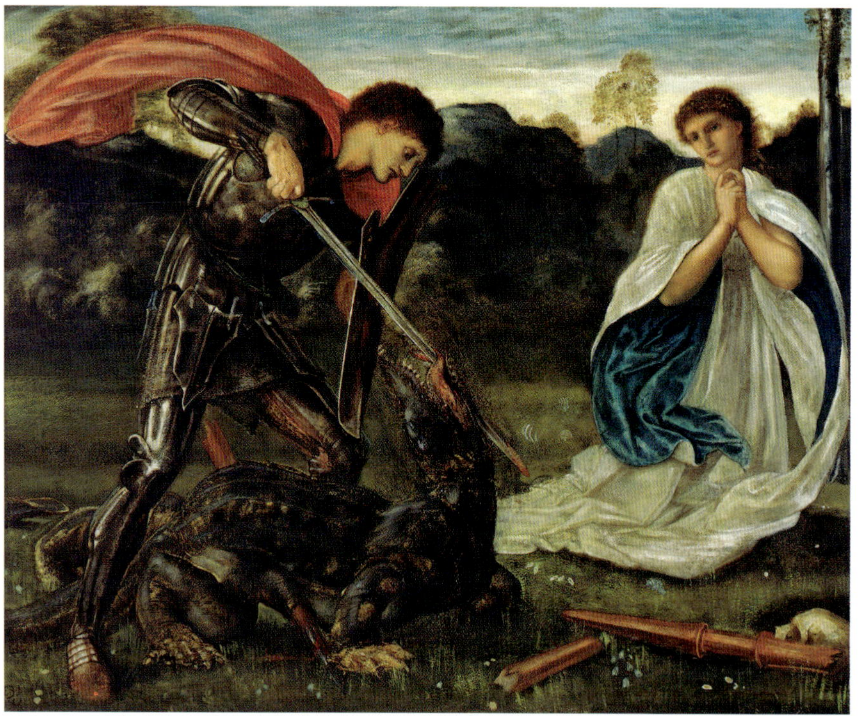

SIR EDWARD COLEY BURNE-JONES (1833-1898)
*The Fight: Saint George kills the Dragon VI* 1864 or 1866
oil on canvas mounted on board 105.4 x 130.8 cm
Art Gallery of New South Wales, gift of Arthur Moon KC 1950

This early work is the sixth in a cycle of seven paintings depicting the *Legend of Saint George* commissioned in 1864 by the watercolour painter Myles Birket Foster for the dining room of his house 'The Hill' at Witley, Surrey. The personification of Christian chivalry, Saint George saves the King's daughter by slaying the dragon to which she has been offered as a human sacrifice. In their gratitude the King and his subjects converted to Christianity. The treatment of the landscape reflects the influence of the Venetian school which was particularly marked in the artist's work of this period.

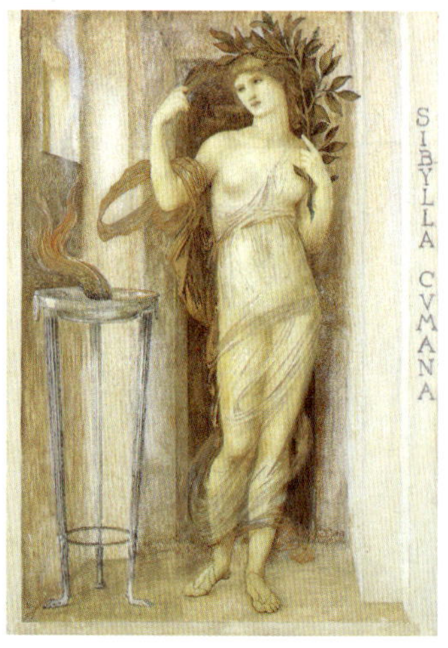


SIR EDWARD COLEY BURNE-JONES
*Sibylla Cumana* 1873
mixed media on paper mounted on cotton cloth
36.8 x 26 cm
Art Gallery of New South Wales, purchased 1970

This figure is related to Burne-Jones's designs for a series of Prophets and Sibyls to be executed in stained glass by Morris & Company in Jesus College Chapel, Cambridge (1873-4). The choice of subjects, as well as the treatment of the figures in the final designs, reflect the influence of Michelangelo's Sistine Chapel decorations which Burne-Jones had studied at length on his recent trip to Italy.

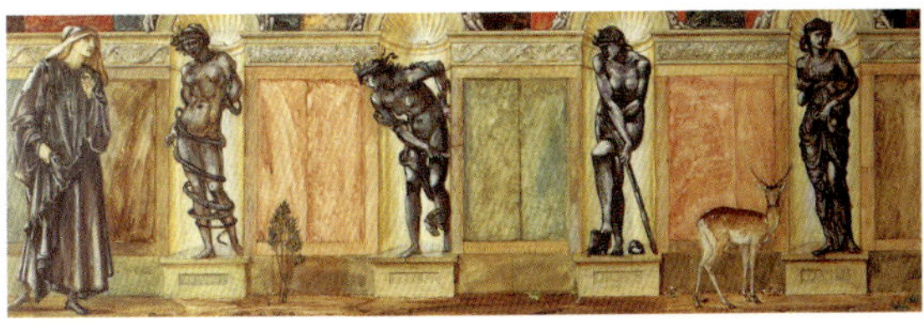

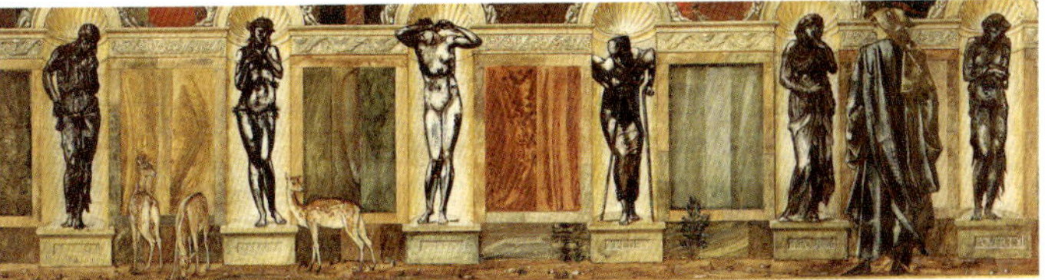

SIR EDWARD COLEY BURNE-JONES
*The Pilgrim at the Garden of Idleness* c.1874
mixed media on paper 30.5 x 89.5 cm and 30.5 x 120.7 cm
John and Julie Schaeffer Collection

In 1874 Burne-Jones began work on a series of designs illustrating Chaucer's *Romaunt of the Rose.* These were to be executed in embroidery as part of the decorations commissioned from Morris & Company by the industrialist Isaac Lowthian for his house Rounton Grange near Northallerton, Yorkshire. The embroideries (now in the William Morris Gallery, Walthamstow) took eight years to complete. Burne-Jones continued to develop the designs in a series of works on paper and oils. This scene, in which the pilgrim gazes on a series of statues representing the miseries of the world (Hate, Felony, Villainy, Covetousness, Avarice, Envy, Sorrow, Age, Time, Hypocrisy and Poverty), is also recorded in large and small versions in oil.

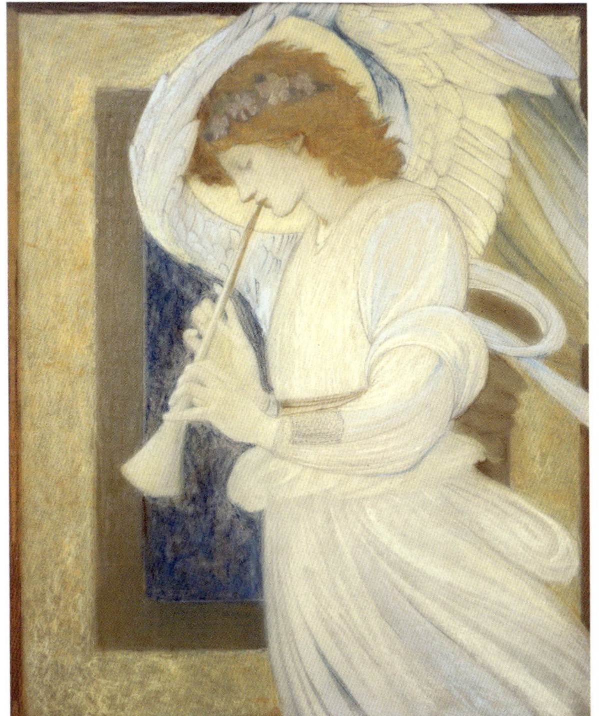

SIR EDWARD COLEY BURNE-JONES
*Angel playing a Flageolet* c.1878
pastel and gouache on paper 73.7 x 60.3 cm
John and Julie Schaeffer Collection

The composition is based on a design for stained glass in the Regimental Chapel in Christ Church Cathedral, Oxford executed by Morris & Company in 1877. A version in watercolour dated 1878, considerably more highly worked than the present example, forms part of the Emma Holt Bequest at Sudley House (National Museums and Galleries on Merseyside). In a lecture given in 1882 Oscar Wilde recalled Burne-Jones's saying to him 'the more materialistic science becomes, the more angels shall I paint: their wings are my protest in favour of the immortality of the soul'.

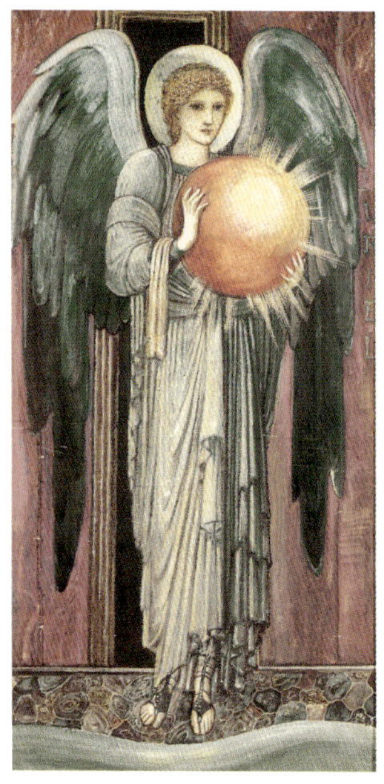

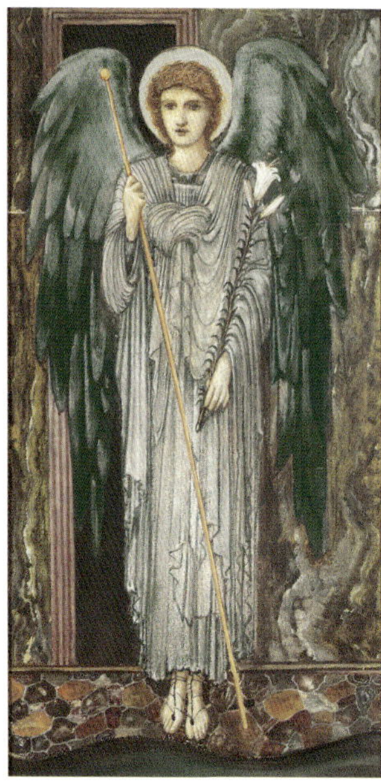

SIR EDWARD COLEY BURNE-JONES
*The Archangel Uriel* and *The Archangel Gabriel*, c.1884
mixed media on paper, each 50.8 x 25.4 cm
John and Julie Schaeffer Collection

In 1881 Burne-Jones received the commission for a series of mosaics to decorate the apse of the American Church in Rome. He conceived a 'Heavenly Jerusalem' with Christ enthroned in the centre and the archangels ranged on either side. The present works appear to have been made after the design had been finalised in 1884 as part of a series of *'ricordi'*. The apse itself was unveiled on Christmas Day 1885. Work continued on the mosaic decoration of the church which became the largest decorative project Burne-Jones ever undertook, though technical difficulties delayed its completion until after his death.

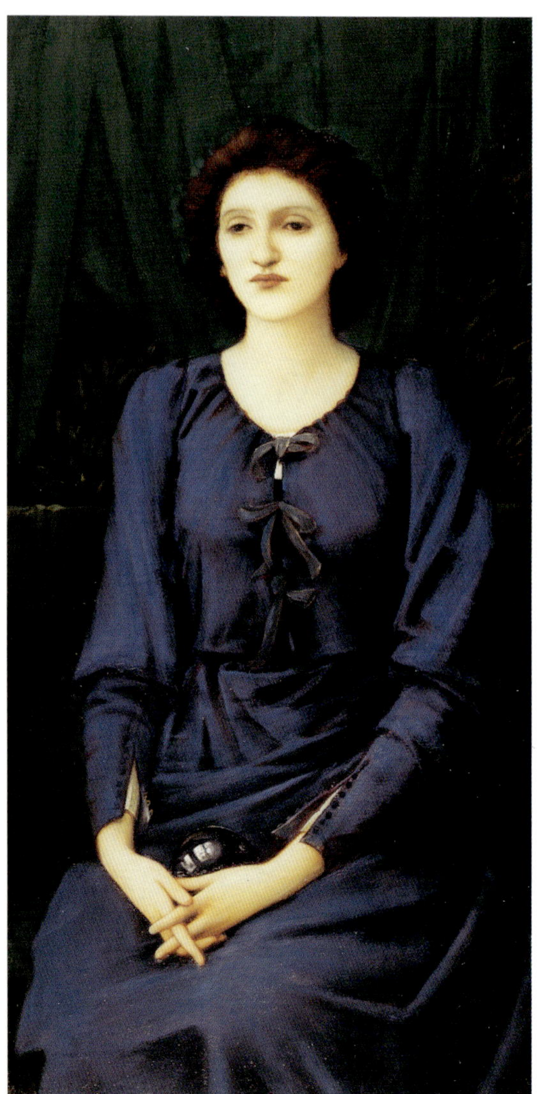

SIR EDWARD COLEY BURNE-JONES
*Portrait of Baronne Madeleine Deslandres* 1896
oil on canvas 116.2 x 58.4 cm
John and Julie Schaeffer Collection

The aristocratic sitter was a novelist, who published under the pseudonym of Ossit. She was a prominent figure among literary and artistic circles in Paris and published an enthusiastic account of Burne-Jones's work in *Le Figaro* in 1893. She commissioned the present portrait from the artist in 1896 and it was exhibited in the Paris Salon in the same year.

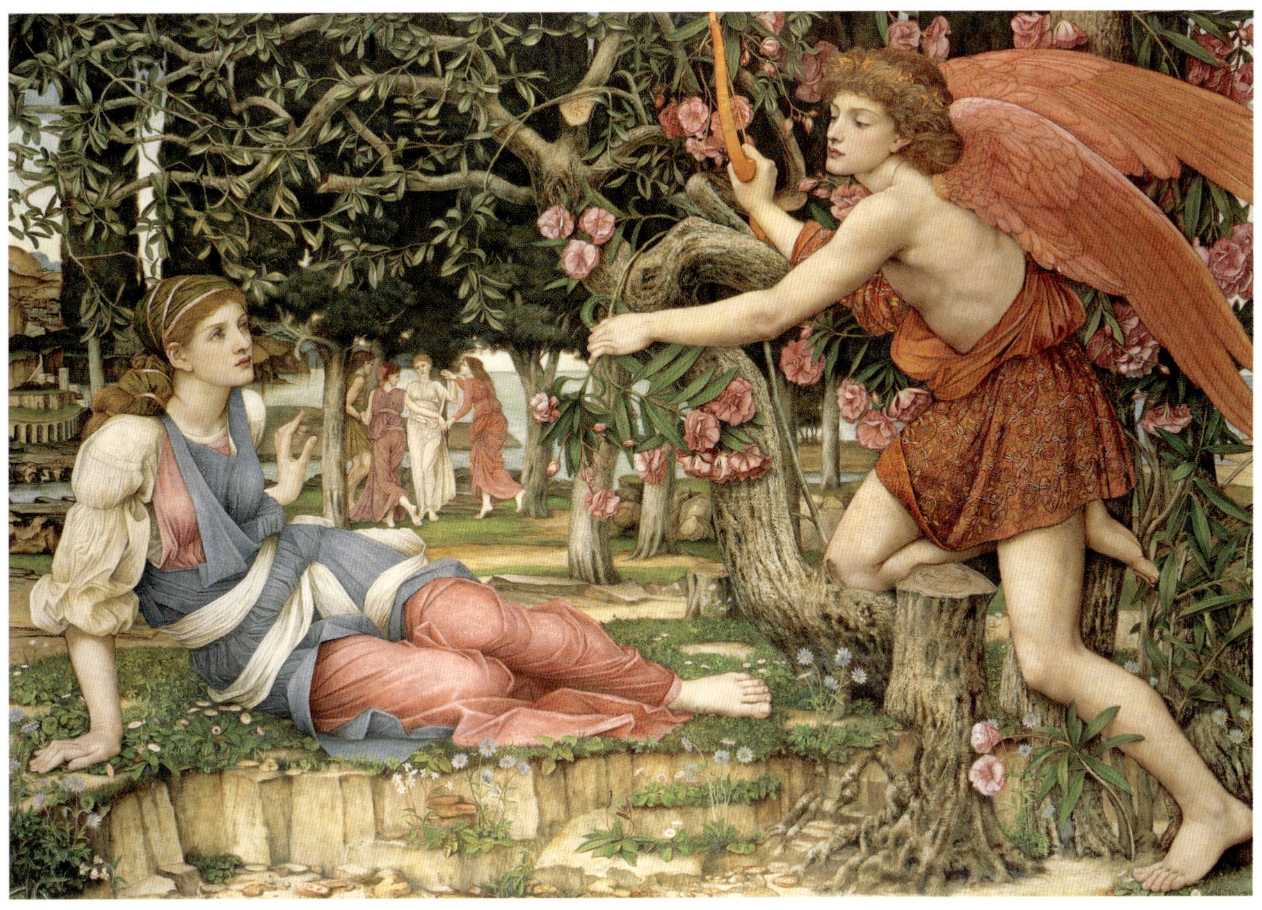

JOHN RODDAM SPENCER STANHOPE (1829-1908)
*Love and the Maiden* 1877
tempera with gold paint and gold leaf on canvas 138 x 202.5 cm
John and Julie Schaeffer Collection

This picture is undoubtedly one of the artist's greatest masterpieces. Painted in Italy, where Stanhope had been living since 1873, it reflects the artist's profound admiration for the work of Botticelli. It is also one of the earliest and most ambitious examples of the nineteenth-century revival of egg-tempera painting. The picture was one of four which Stanhope sent to the inaugural exhibition of the Grosvenor Gallery in Bond Street in 1877 which in effect launched the Aesthetic Movement. Stanhope's works were shown alongside those of Burne-Jones and attracted favourable comment from such distinguished critics as Henry James and the young Oscar Wilde.

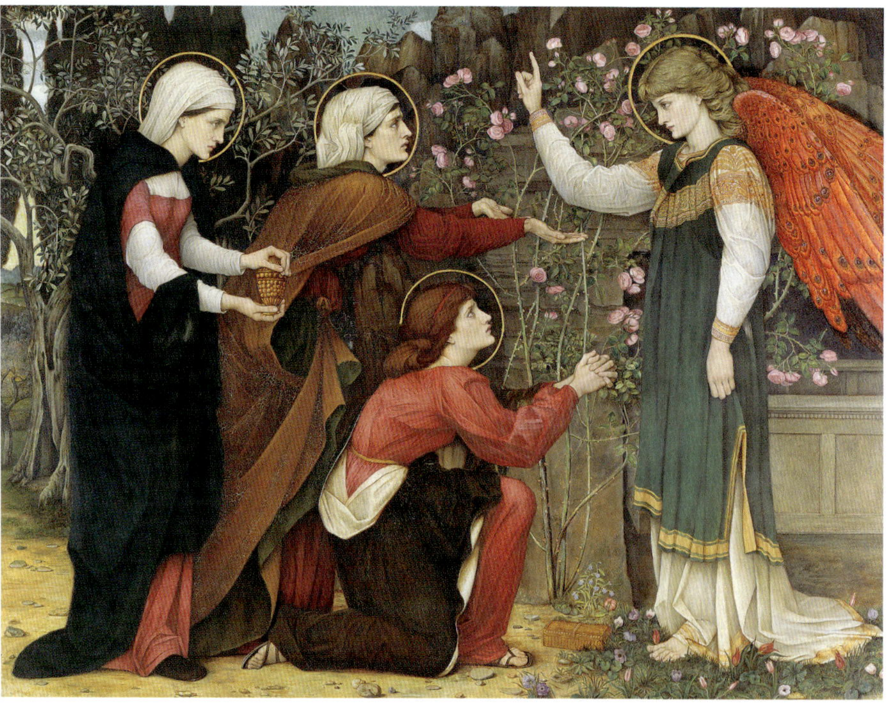

JOHN RODDAM SPENCER STANHOPE
*Why seek ye the Living among the Dead?* mid-1870s or c.1890?
oil, gesso, gold leaf, wax medium on canvas 129.8 x 168.8 cm
Art Gallery of New South Wales, gift of Arthur Moon KC 1950

In Italy Stanhope became interested in mural painting and in 1872-9 he undertook a series of fresco panels for the chapel of Marlborough College, Wiltshire, representing the Ministrations of the Angels. The Sydney picture is a repetition in oil of one of these panels. The title is a quotation from the gospel of Luke: when the three Maries arrived to anoint the dead body of Christ, they found the stone rolled away from the sepulchre and ' ...two men stood by them in shining garments: And ... said unto them, Why seek ye the living among the dead?: He is not here but is risen'. Stanhope in fact follows Matthew's account in showing only one angel.

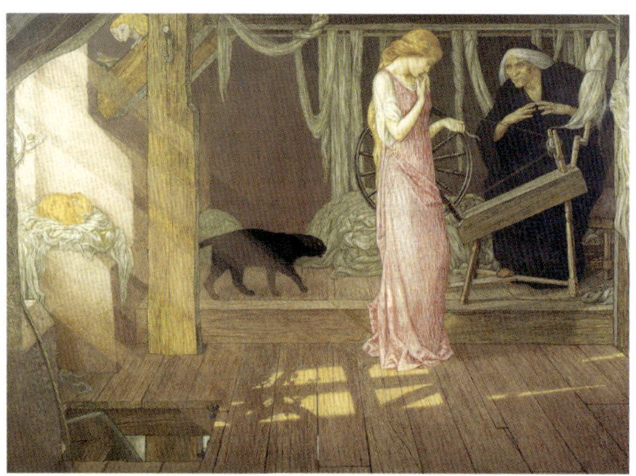

JOHN DICKSON BATTEN (1860-1932)
*Sleeping Beauty: the Princess pricks her Finger*
tempera on board 76 x 103 cm
John and Julie Schaeffer Collection

Batten began his career as a barrister, but decided to train as a painter shortly after being called to the bar in 1884. He worked as a book illustrator as well as a painter and many of his works illustrate fairy tales. Along with Spencer Stanhope he was one of the principal artists involved in the revival of egg tempera as a painting medium. Both artists were among those who founded the Society of Painters in Tempera in 1901.

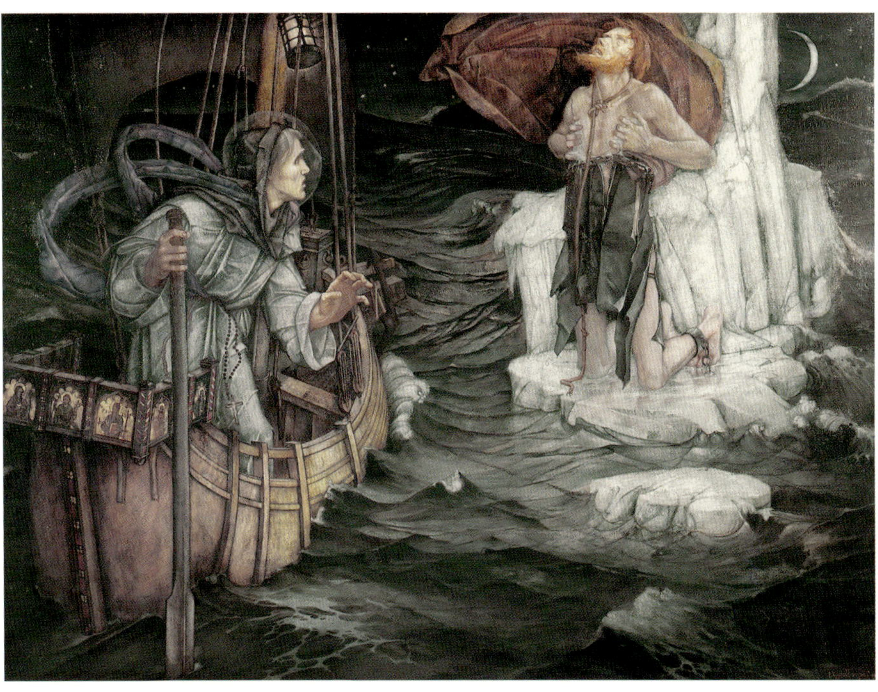

EDWARD REGINALD FRAMPTON (1872-1923)
*The Voyage of Saint Brendan* 1908
oil on canvas 132 x 183 cm
John and Julie Schaeffer Collection

Frampton practised a highly decorative and somewhat mannered style which owes much to the example of Burne-Jones. The subject of this picture is taken from Matthew Arnold's poem *St Brendan* first published in 1860. Brendan was an Irish monk of the 6th century who is said to have sailed the seas for seven years in search of paradise. In this scene he encounters the tormented figure of Judas Iscariot chained to an iceberg.

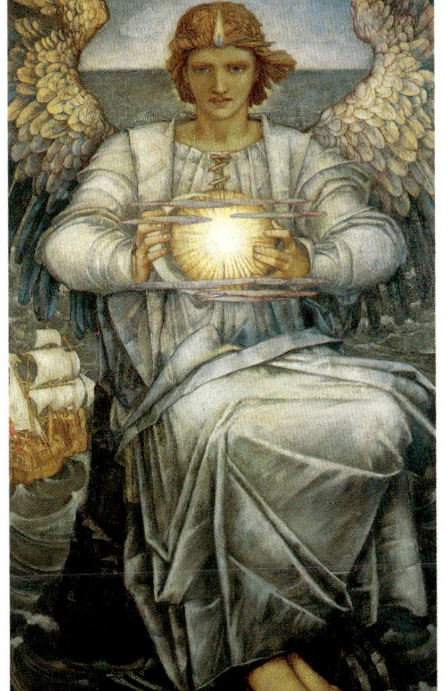

EDWARD REGINALD FRAMPTON
*The Angel of the Sea* c.1905?
oil on canvas 121.9 x 68.6 cm
John and Julie Schaeffer Collection

Frampton was noted for his decorative murals, both ecclesiastical and secular. The upper half of the figure in this picture is virtually an exact repetition of an angel in the artist's wall decorations in All Saints' Church, Hastings (completed c.1905). The artist was a keen sailor and many of his works have marine or nautical themes.

# WATTS

……

Apart from his infrequent attendances at the Royal Academy Schools from 1835, Watts received no formal training as a painter. After first exhibiting at the Royal Academy in 1837 he went on to win a premium in the first competition for decorations in the new Palace of Westminster held in 1843. This provided him with the funds to visit Italy and in Florence he stayed for nearly four years as the guest of Lord and Lady Holland. In Italy he learnt fresco technique and applied himself to the study of the great masters of the Italian Renaissance, above all Raphael and Michelangelo.

Returning to London in 1847 Watts again won a premium in the Palace of Westminster competition of that year. From 1851 he became firmly ensconced in the household of Thoby and Sara Prinsep at Little Holland House where he was provided with his own studio. Mrs Prinsep's hospitality attracted an artistic and literary circle which included such prominent figures as Tennyson and Dickens as well as painters, such as Leighton, Millais, Rossetti and Burne-Jones and the photographer Julia Margaret Cameron.

Watts was nothing if not ambitious. Most of his creative energies were channelled into a series of earnest subject pictures which became increasingly 'symbolical' in character. One of his ambitions was to revive the art of mural painting in England and he undertook a number of fresco commissions in the 1850s and early 1860s notably in the Great Hall at Lincoln's Inn. He also worked for most of his life on his project for a 'House of Life' comprising a series of frescoes symbolizing the history of mankind, though the frescoes themselves were never begun. In the late 1860s he also took up sculpture undertaking some projects on a monumental scale, such as his *Physical Energy* in Kensington Gardens begun c.1883.

Watts was elected an associate of the Royal Academy in 1867 and became an Academician later in the same year. Throughout his career he was an subtle and incisive portrait painter, but it was in his subject pictures that he sought and finally achieved an international reputation. This was established in exhibitions of his work held at the Royal Institution in Manchester in 1880, at the Grosvenor Gallery in 1881-2 and at the Metropolitan Museum in New York in 1884-5. His works were also well known in Paris where they were shown at the Exposition Universelle of 1878 and the Salon of 1880. In addition he made several gifts of paintings to public institutions: his series of portraits of eminent men to the National Portrait Gallery, London, twenty-three allegorical paintings to the Tate Gallery, and others to museums in America, Canada and France.

Watts has generally been admired more for his portraits than his subject pictures, but especially in recent years his reputation has been considerably revived as one of the leading figures in the emergence of the Symbolist movement.

• **George Frederic Watts** *Love and Life* 1884 (detail)

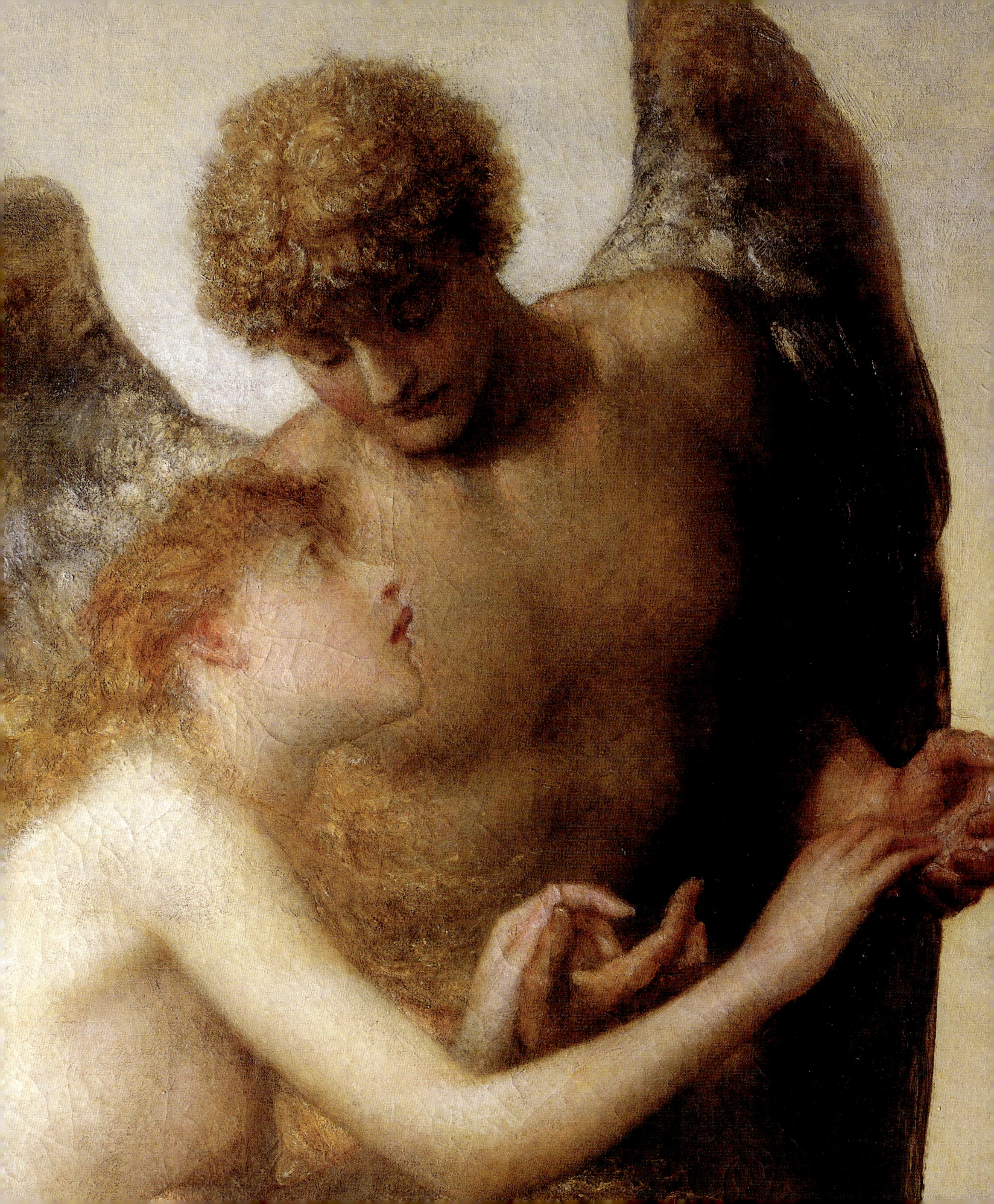

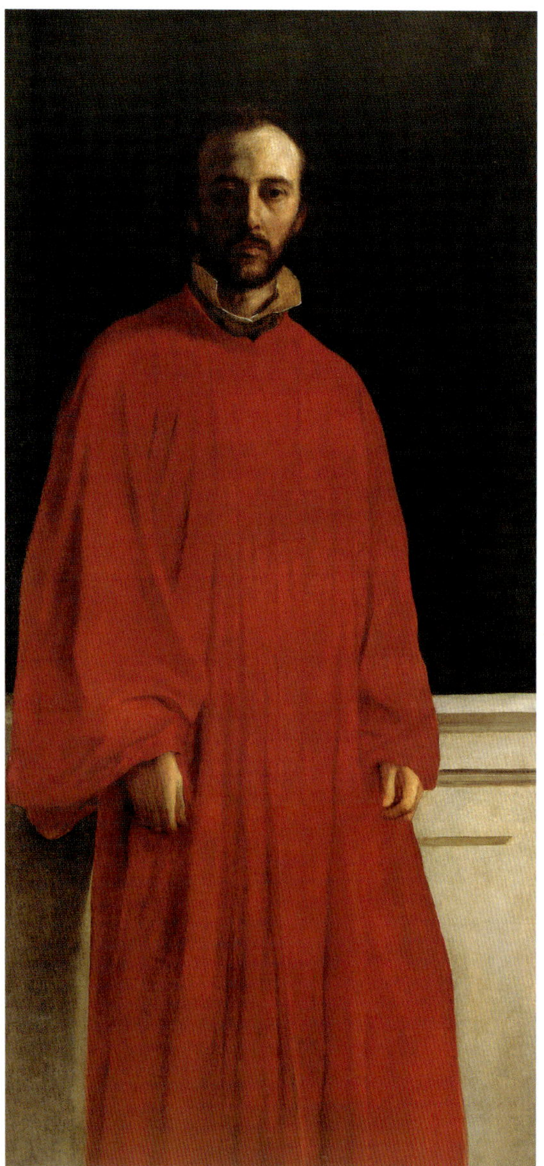

GEORGE FREDERIC WATTS (1817-1904)
*Self-Portrait* 1853
oil on canvas 152.4 x 72.4 cm
John and Julie Schaeffer Collection

Watts made numerous self-portraits. 'I paint myself constantly', he wrote, 'that is to say whenever I want to make an experiment in method or colour and am not in the humour to make a design'. This picture was painted shortly after the artist moved into Little Holland House where the hospitable Mrs Prinsep provided him with a studio. It shows the artist wearing the floor-length robe which was his customary (and unconventional) attire at the period. It was hung, unframed, outside his studio.

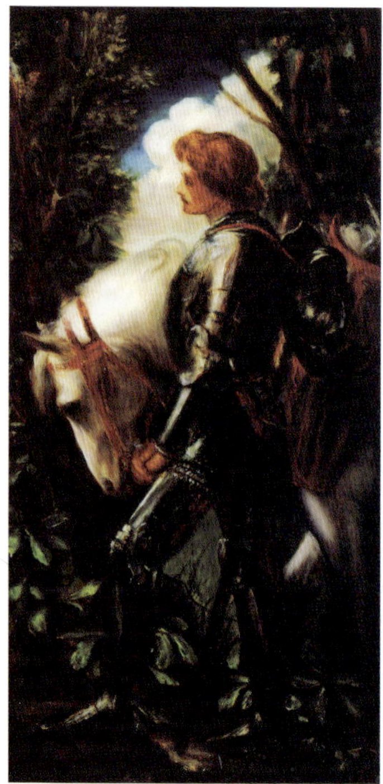

GEORGE FREDERIC WATTS
*Sir Galahad* c.1862
oil on canvas 54.3 x 27.3 cm
John and Julie Schaeffer Collection

The picture is almost an exact repetition of one exhibited by Watts at the Royal Academy in 1862. The medieval, chivalric theme is unusual in Watts's work and was doubtless inspired by Rossetti and Burne-Jones with whom he would have come into contact at Little Holland House.

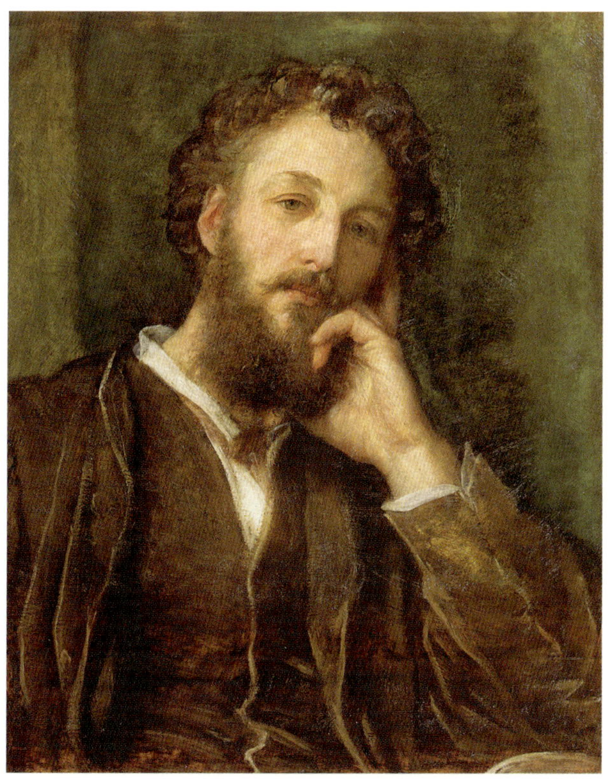

GEORGE FREDERIC WATTS
*Portrait of Frederic Leighton* 1871
oil on canvas 66 x 53 cm
John and Julie Schaeffer Collection

In the early 1850s Watts began painting a series of portraits of eminent contemporaries many of whom were Mrs Prinsep's guests at Little Holland House. Leighton was to become a particularly close friend. In 1875 Watts built himself a house in Melbury Road on a plot adjoining Leighton's house, a gate between the two gardens providing informal access from one to the other. This sensitive and humane portrait, with its restrained palette and loose brushwork is in marked contrast to Leighton's official *Self-portrait* (see p.37).

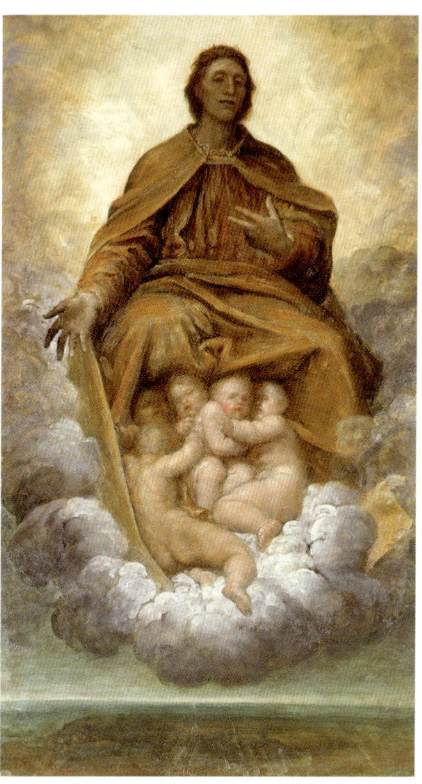

GEORGE FREDERIC WATTS
*The Spirit of Christianity* 1873-5
oil on canvas 68.5 x 38 cm
John and Julie Schaeffer Collection

In 1872-5 Watts painted four versions of this subject. He attempted to express the 'symbol of compassionate tenderness … an idea that may be accepted by all Christian Churches' or in other words 'the Spirit of Religion … in contradiction to the extreme importance attributed to dogmas which appear to me to be mostly unimportant'. The present version was acquired by the artist's friend and most important patron, Charles H. Rickards, the Manchester industrialist and philanthropist.

GEORGE FREDERIC WATTS
*Love and Life* 1884
oil on canvas 222.5 x 123.5 cm
John and Julie Schaeffer Collection

The subject is explained by the artist's friend and biographer Mrs Russell Barrington: 'Love is leading the way, and helping Life, by his support and tenderness, to climb the difficult path – emblematic of the struggling conditions which more or less, are the portion of all human existence'. The picture was presented by the artist to the American nation in 1894 and was to be displayed in the White House, but for the intervention of Mrs Emily D. Martin (National Superintendent of Purity in Literature and Art for the Women's Christian Temperance Union) who objected to the nudity of the figures. In 1902, disregarding Mrs Martin's renewed remonstrances Theodore Roosevelt had the picture hung in the White House and it remained there until 1932.

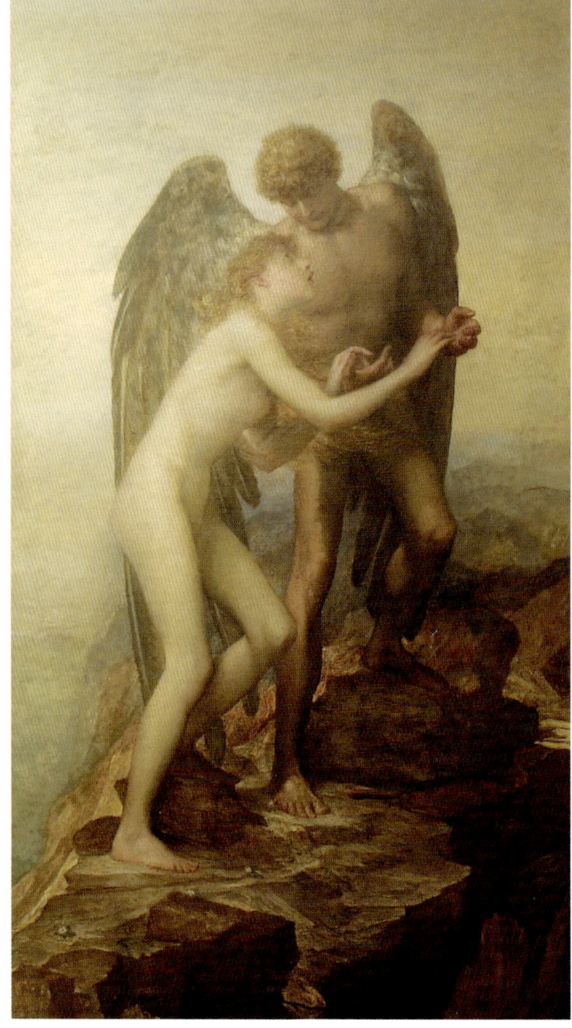

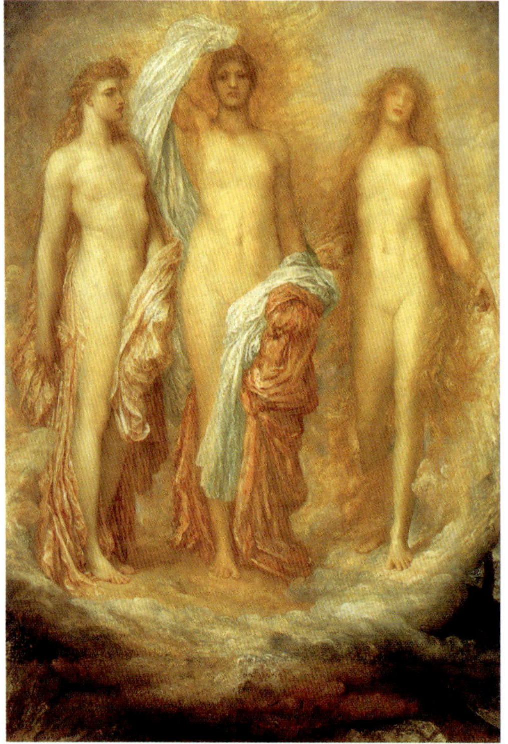

GEORGE FREDERIC WATTS
*Olympus on Ida (The Judgment of Paris)* 1885
oil on canvas 147 x 102.2 cm
John and Julie Schaeffer Collection

The subject is the beauty contest on Mount Ida between the goddesses Minerva, Juno and Venus. The shepherd Paris, who was called on to pass judgment, is absent in Watts's image. When the artist wrote to the painting's first owner he referred to it as '… quite one of the best I have ever painted. I have tried to express without attributes the different characteristics of the three goddesses and by the colour and quality of surface to suggest a certain sense of the celestial perfume accompanying them'.

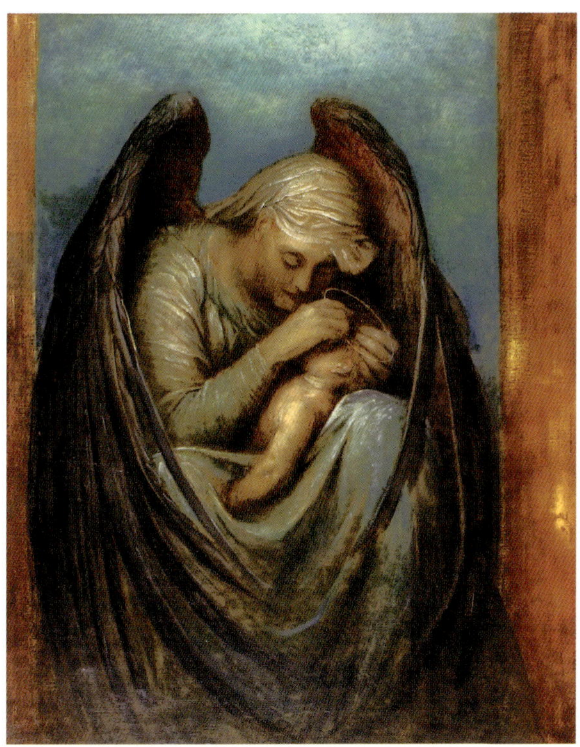

GEORGE FREDERIC WATTS
*Death crowning Innocence* c.1889
oil on canvas 127 x 102 cm
John and Julie Schaeffer Collection

The design was first conceived in 1886. Watts's fiancée, Mary Tytler, was then staying at the family home in Scotland prior to their marriage in November. In October after a serious illness occasioned by a riding accident a young nephew of hers died. 'I am making a design', Watts wrote in response to this news, 'which hereafter may be lovingly worked into a monument, the Angel of Death with a child in her lap on whose head she is placing a circlet …'. This is a later version of that picture.

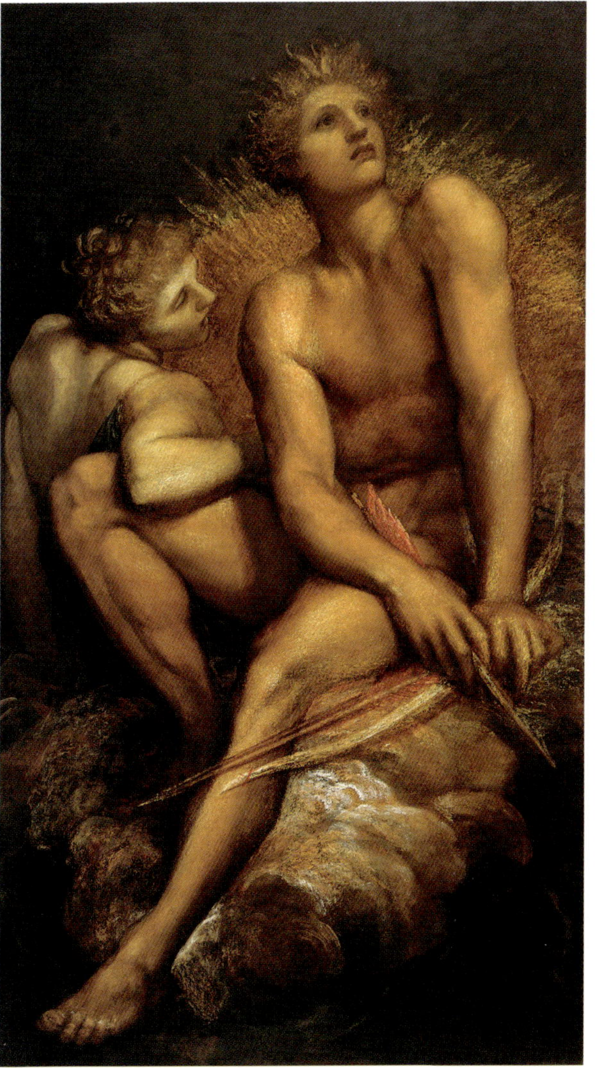

GEORGE FREDERIC WATTS
*Artemis and Hyperion* 1880s?
oil on canvas 213.4 x 124.5 cm
Art Gallery of New South Wales, purchased 1983

In Mrs Watts's manuscript catalogue of her husband's works the subject is described as follows: 'A nature-myth of the Greek poets, Hyperion representing the sun and Artemis his sister, the moon who loved the Titan Orion'. The picture is a later version of a painting exhibited at the Grosvenor Gallery in 1881-2 and was never considered to be finished. The model for Hyperion is said to have been Arthur Prinsep, son of the Prinseps with whom Watts lived at Little Holland House.

# LEIGHTON

……

Leighton was born in Scarborough. Most of his childhood, however, was spent on the continent in Germany, Switzerland and Italy. In 1846 his family settled in Frankfurt and there he became a pupil at the Städelsches Kunstinstitut studying under the Nazarene painter Edward von Steinle. In 1852 when his mother and father returned to England, Leighton travelled to Italy and established himself in Rome. Among his artist friends were the landscape painters Giovanni Costa and George Hemming Mason who were later to become leading figures in the 'Etruscan' school of landscape painters.

In Rome Leighton began work on the canvas which brought him his first spectacular success. This was a huge painting showing Cimabue processing through the streets of Florence with his newly-painted *Madonna*, the young Giotto at his side (Royal Collection, on loan to the National Gallery, London). The painting was shown at the Royal Academy exhibition of 1855 and was purchased by Queen Victoria, an astounding honour for a hitherto unknown young artist. In spite of his success in London Leighton decided to pursue his artistic training in Paris where he was based for another four years. There he met the elderly Ingres and Delacroix and admired the works of many contemporary artists including Couture and Robert-Fleury as well as the Dutch painter Ary Scheffer.

He finally returned to London in 1859 and set about following up on the triumph of *Cimabue's Madonna*, though initially with little success. Although he was in close contact with Rossetti and Burne-Jones, his art now evolved in a new direction. During the 1860s he developed the sensuous classicising idiom which would be characteristic of his art for the rest of his career. The key example of this new approach was his second great processional painting of *The Syracusan Bride* which caused a sensation at the Royal Academy exhibition in 1866. The course of Leighton's development was in the artist's own words a 'passage from Gothicism to Classicism'. From now on his Gods were Greek and the scene was set for a hugely successful career.

By the time that Burne-Jones launched onto the British art scene his own brand of Pre-Raphaelitism in the Grosvenor House exhibition of 1877, Leighton had achieved a position of undisputed pre-eminence. In the following year, at the age of 38, he was elected President of the Royal Academy. In the last two decades of his career, he produced a succession of major works which while classical in inspiration constitute as important a contribution to the Victorian Aesthetic movement as those of Burne-Jones. Both artists were fundamentally concerned with the pursuit of beauty and in Leighton's vision perfect beauty was to be sought in a distant past and under a Mediterranean sun. Frequently his works are without literary subject matter of any kind. Everyday events take place in a remote and unspecific dream-world on which dust never settles. Such works lack the moral dimension of French neoclassicism: they are not to do with acts of heroism, but with visions of beauty.

Leighton's reputation declined dramatically in the twentieth century. When his most celebrated work, *Flaming June* (now Museo de Arte, Ponce), was rediscovered in 1963 it was offered for sale for £50. The picture is now regarded as one of the masterpieces of Victorian art.

• **Frederic, Lord Leighton** *The Syracusan Bride Leading Wild Beasts in Procession to the Temple of Diana* 1865-6 (detail)

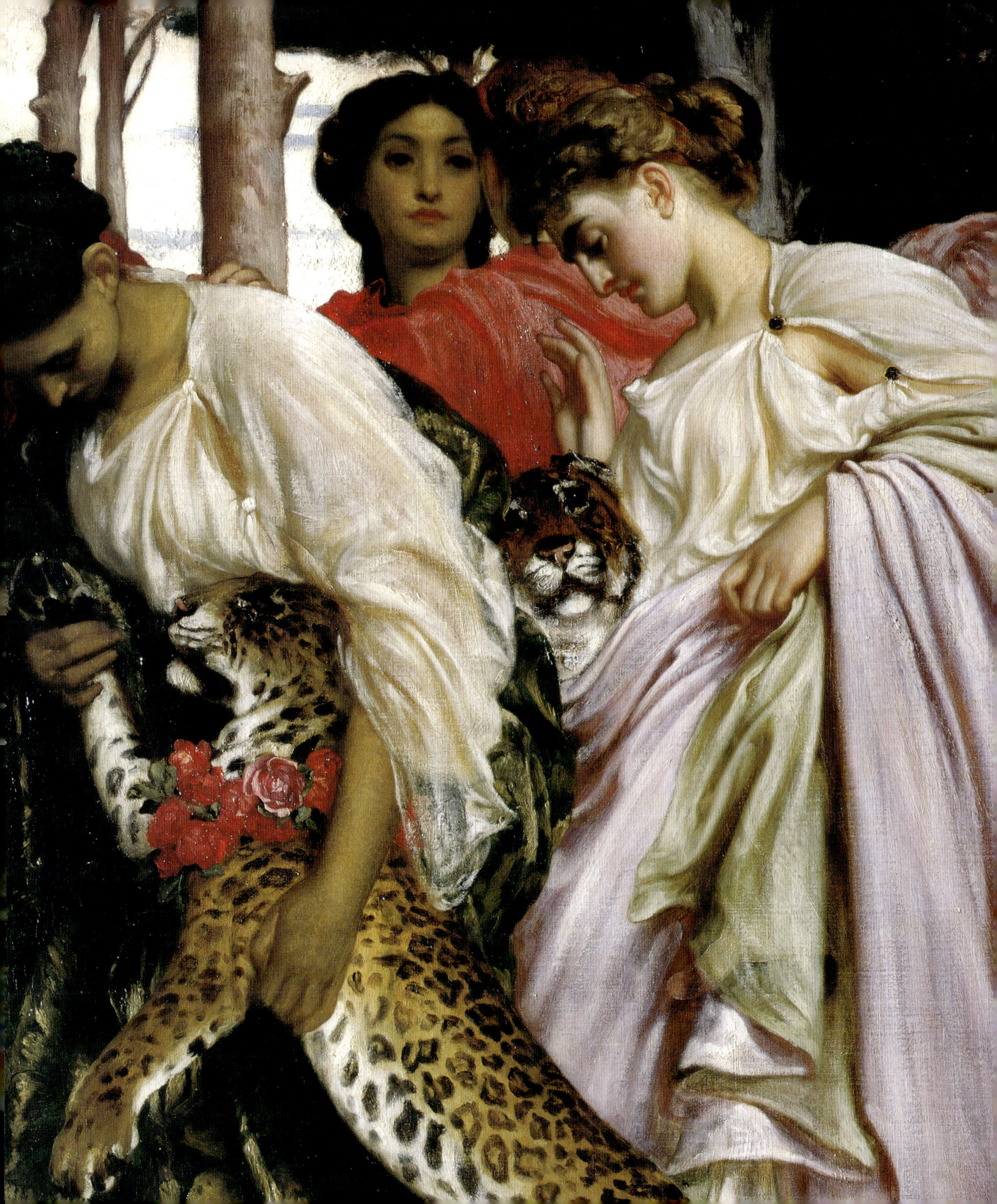

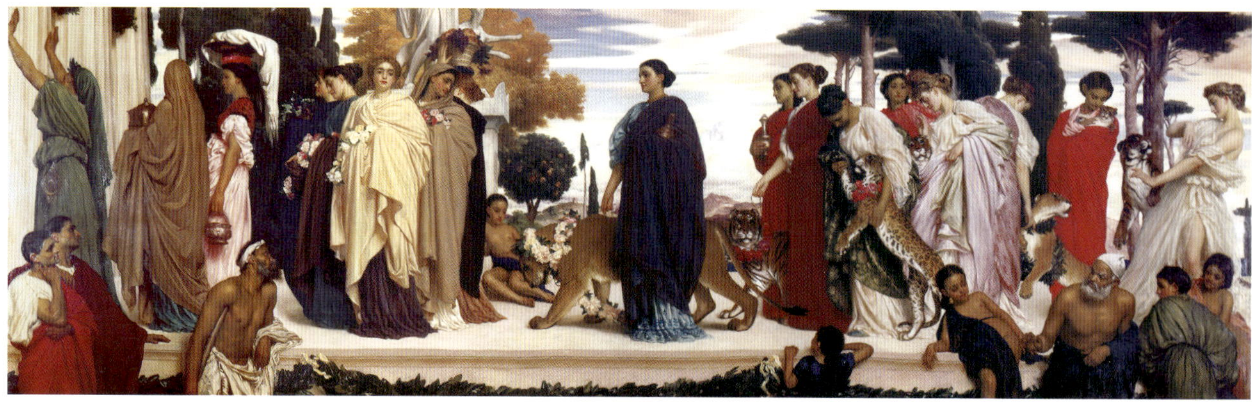

FREDERIC, LORD LEIGHTON (1830-1896)
*The Syracusan Bride Leading Wild Beasts in Procession to the Temple of Diana (subject suggested by a passage in the second "Idyll" of Theocritus, 'And for her then many other wild beasts were going in procession')* 1865-6
oil on canvas 133.5 x 424.3 cm
John and Julie Schaeffer Collection

One of Leighton's largest and most ambitious works, this vast canvas is the second of the artist's great processional paintings. In it he hoped to repeat the success of *Cimabue's Madonna* which had been acquired by Queen Victoria ten years earlier. Begun in 1865, the Syracusan Bride was only with some difficulty completed in time for the Royal Academy Exhibition of 1866. It marks a major staging post in Leighton's career which henceforth would be predominantly dedicated to classical themes. The subject of the picture is substantially the artist's own invention being merely suggested by an inconsequential line from Theocritus which Leighton quotes in parentheses in the full title.

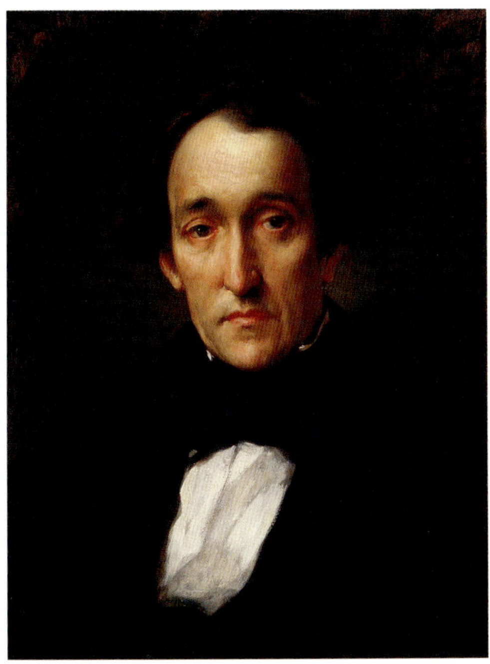

FREDERIC, LORD LEIGHTON
*Portrait of the Artist's Father* probably mid-1850s
oil on canvas 61 x 46 cm
John and Julie Schaeffer Collection

Leighton's background was both wealthy and intellectual. His grandfather was a successful society doctor in St Petersburg and physician to the Tsarin. It was in St Petersburg that Leighton's father, Dr Frederic Septimus, worked before going up to Edinburgh University to study medicine, finally completing his studies in Paris. By all accounts he was an austerely intellectual man and he acted himself as tutor to his children as the family moved around Europe settling periodically in France, Switzerland, Germany and Italy. 'He strongly discountenanced the idea of my being an artist', Leighton later recalled, 'unless I could be eminent in Art'.

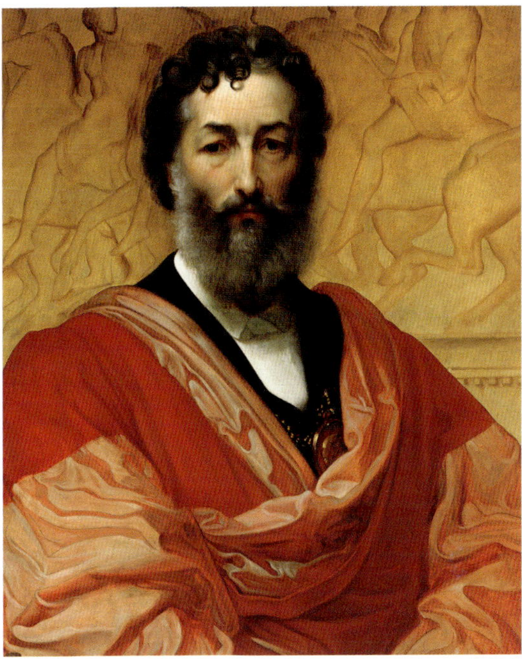

PAOLO FOSSI (AFTER LEIGHTON)
*Portrait of Frederic Lord Leighton, after the Artist's Uffizi Self-Portrait* c.1880
oil on canvas 77 x 64 cm
John and Julie Schaeffer Collection

Leighton was honoured in 1880 by the request to provide his own contribution to the famous collection of artists' self-portraits in the Uffizi, Florence. A number of replicas of the picture were made of which the example in the Schaeffer collection was given by the artist to cousins in Shropshire. Leighton is shown in academic robes reflecting the honorary degrees which he had been awarded by the Universities of Oxford, Cambridge and Edinburgh in 1879. He wears the gold medal of President of the Royal Academy, while in the background is a section of the cast of the Parthenon frieze which he had in his own studio.

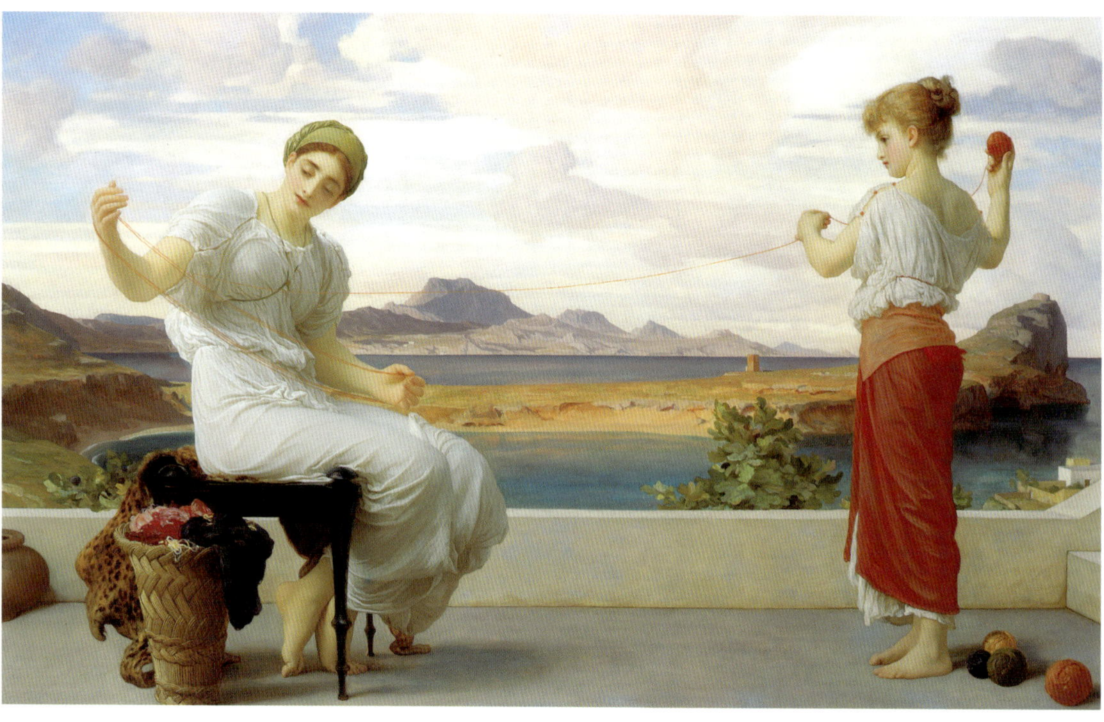

FREDERIC, LORD LEIGHTON
*Winding the Skein* c.1878
oil on canvas 100.3 x 161.3 cm
Art Gallery of New South Wales, purchased 1974

Leighton translates the domestic activity of winding balls of wool into an idyllic vision of classical antiquity set against the Bay of Lindos on the island of Rhodes. The landscape is based on sketches made on the site in 1867, an example of which is in the Gallery's collection (see below). In 1877 Leighton made a further trip this time to Spain to find the sky effect for this picture, but he failed to find that 'clear, keen autumn weather … which I had the right to demand of a Mediterranean October'.

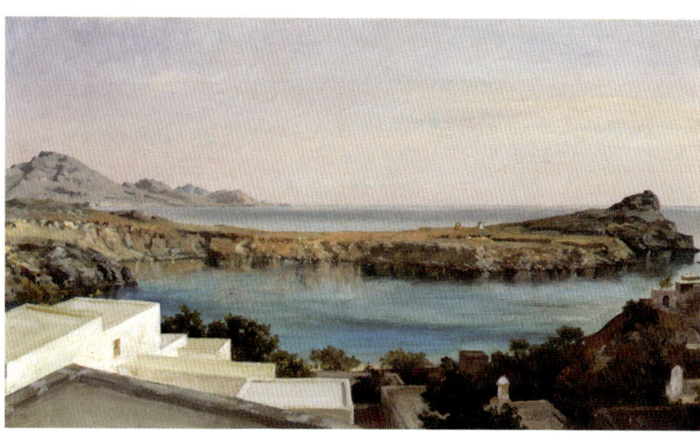

FREDERIC, LORD LEIGHTON
*Lindos, Rhodes* 1867
oil on canvas 25.7 x 45.4 cm
Art Gallery of New South Wales, purchased 1990

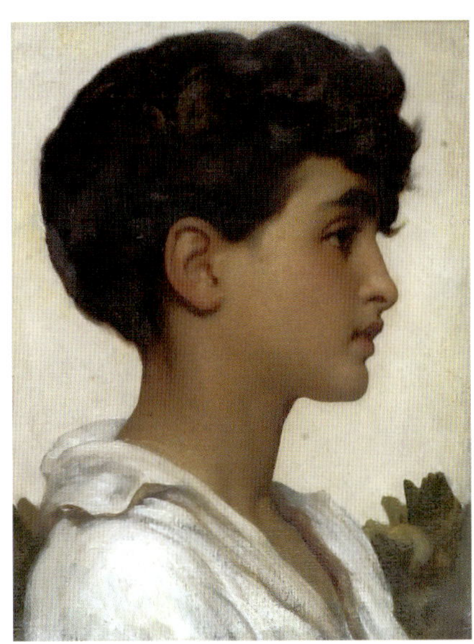

FREDERIC, LORD LEIGHTON
*Paolo* 1875
oil on canvas 26 x 20 cm
John and Julie Schaeffer Collection

One of the most appealing of Leighton's small-scale figure studies, this work shows a young Italian boy, Paolo, who served as a model to the artist on at least two occasions during his visit to the island of Capri in 1875. The picture is not in fact a study for a larger painting, but a finished work in its own right. The fact that Leighton treated it as such is demonstrated by his sending it for exhibition at the Royal Academy in 1876.

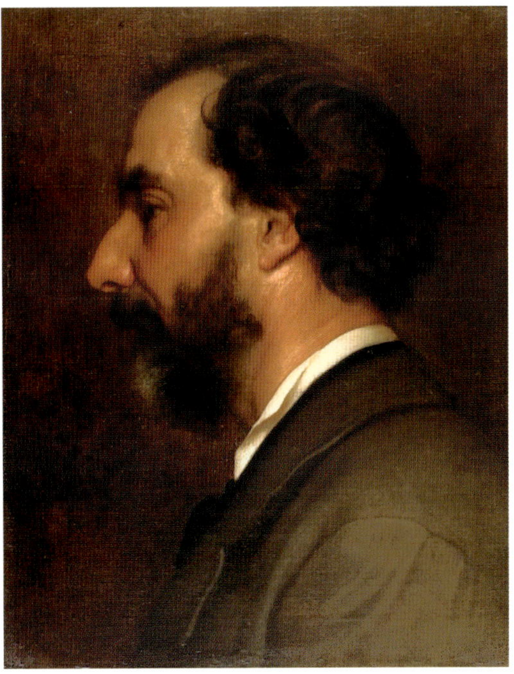

FREDERIC, LORD LEIGHTON
*Portrait of Professor Giovanni Costa* 1878
oil on canvas 48.5 x 39 cm
John and Julie Schaeffer Collection

Giovanni Costa was a landscape painter and the leading figure of the so-called 'Etruscan school'. Leighton met him first in 1853 in Rome and the painters became close friends exchanging visits between London and Rome. This portrait was painted in the autumn of 1878 while Leighton was staying with Costa at Lerici on the Ligurian coast. It was exhibited at the Royal Academy in the following year, the first in which Leighton exhibited as President of the Academy.

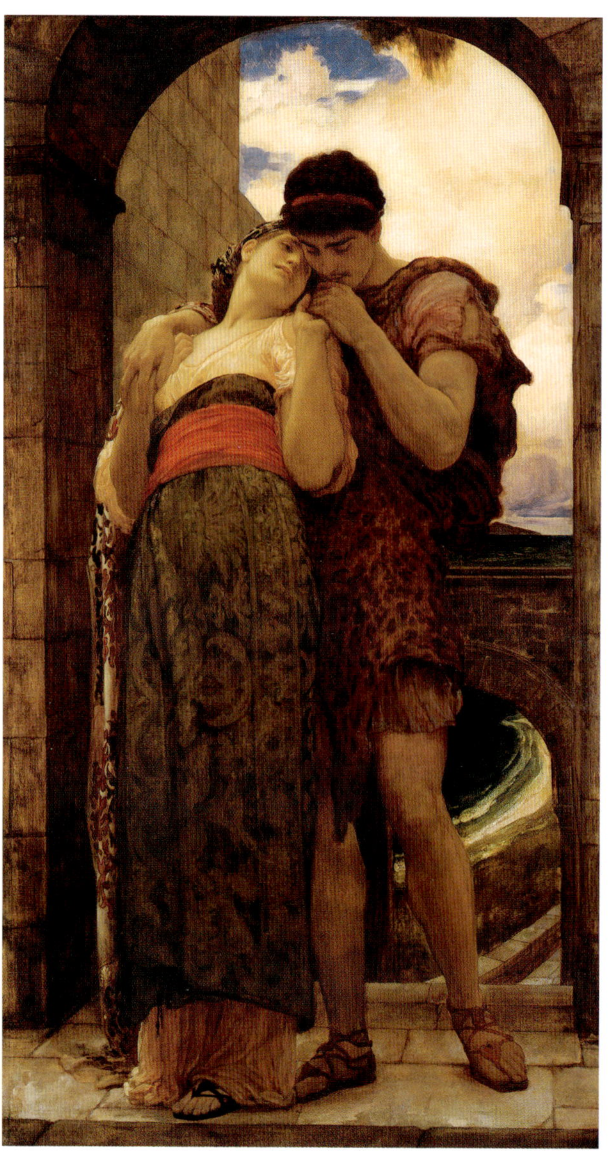

FREDERIC, LORD LEIGHTON
*Wedded* 1882
oil on canvas mounted on board 145.4 x 81.3 cm
Art Gallery of New South Wales, purchased 1882

The setting is an archway of the ruined Greek theatre at Taormina in Sicily. According to one of his early biographers 'Wedded ranks as Leighton's most generally popular picture'. The image became familiar in engraved reproduction and the figures were also repeated in a bronze statue by Giambattista Amendola. It was on seeing this picture that Robert Browning is said to have remarked, 'I find a poetry in that man's work I can find in no other'.

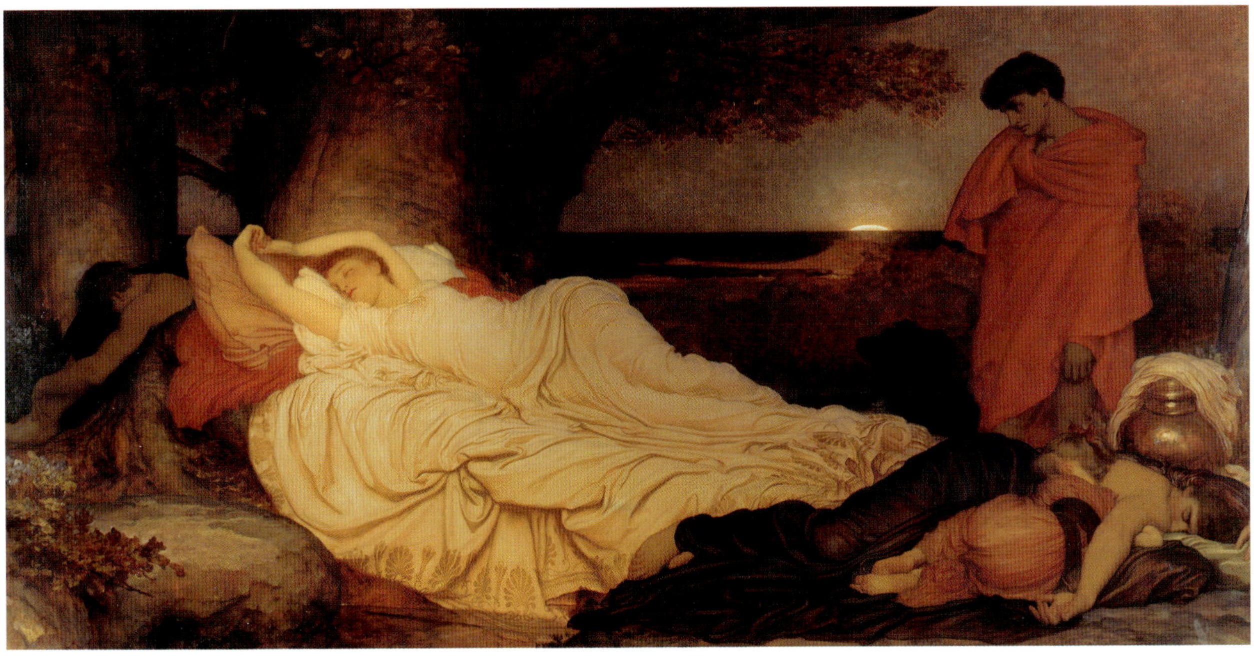

FREDERIC, LORD LEIGHTON
*Cymon and Iphigenia* 1884
oil on canvas 163 x 328 cm
Art Gallery of New South Wales, purchased 1976

The subject is from Boccaccio's *Decameron* where the tale is told of a certain Galesus. He was the handsomest son of a noble Cypriot named Aristippus, but so uncouth and uneducated that he was known as Cymon (meaning "brute"). One Spring afternoon he came across a girl, Iphigenia, asleep with her slaves in a meadow and became transfixed by her beauty. His love for Iphigenia caused Cymon to abandon his boorish ways and to acquire the accomplishments fitting to the true nobility of his soul. Leighton changes the time of day to that which he described as 'the most mysteriously beautiful in the whole twenty-four hours, when the merest lip of the moon has risen from behind the sea horizon …'. The rising moon may be taken as a symbol for the enlightenment of Cymon's soul.

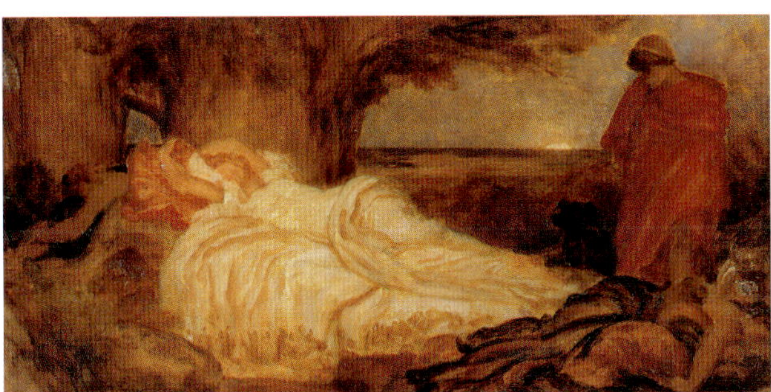

FREDERIC, LORD LEIGHTON
*Colour Study for Cymon and Iphigenia* 1884
oil on canvas 23.5 x 46.5 cm
Art Gallery of New South Wales, purchased 1986

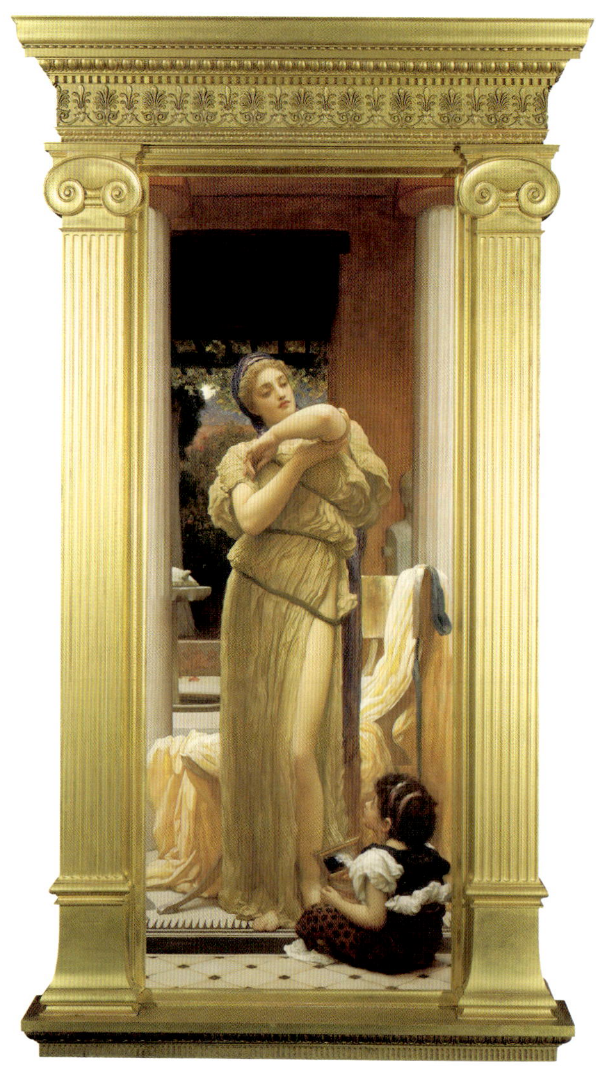

FREDERIC, LORD LEIGHTON
*The Bracelet* c.1894
oil on canvas 153 x 59.7 cm
John and Julie Schaeffer Collection

Leighton submitted this work to the Royal Academy exhibition of 1894, two years before his death and it was again included in the posthumous retrospective held at the same institution in 1897. The picture is an evocation, without mythological subject or apparent symbolic intent, of a domestic scene in classical Greece. With its dominant yellow-orange tonality the picture is a strong reminder of Leighton's leanings toward the Aestheticism of an artist such as Whistler.

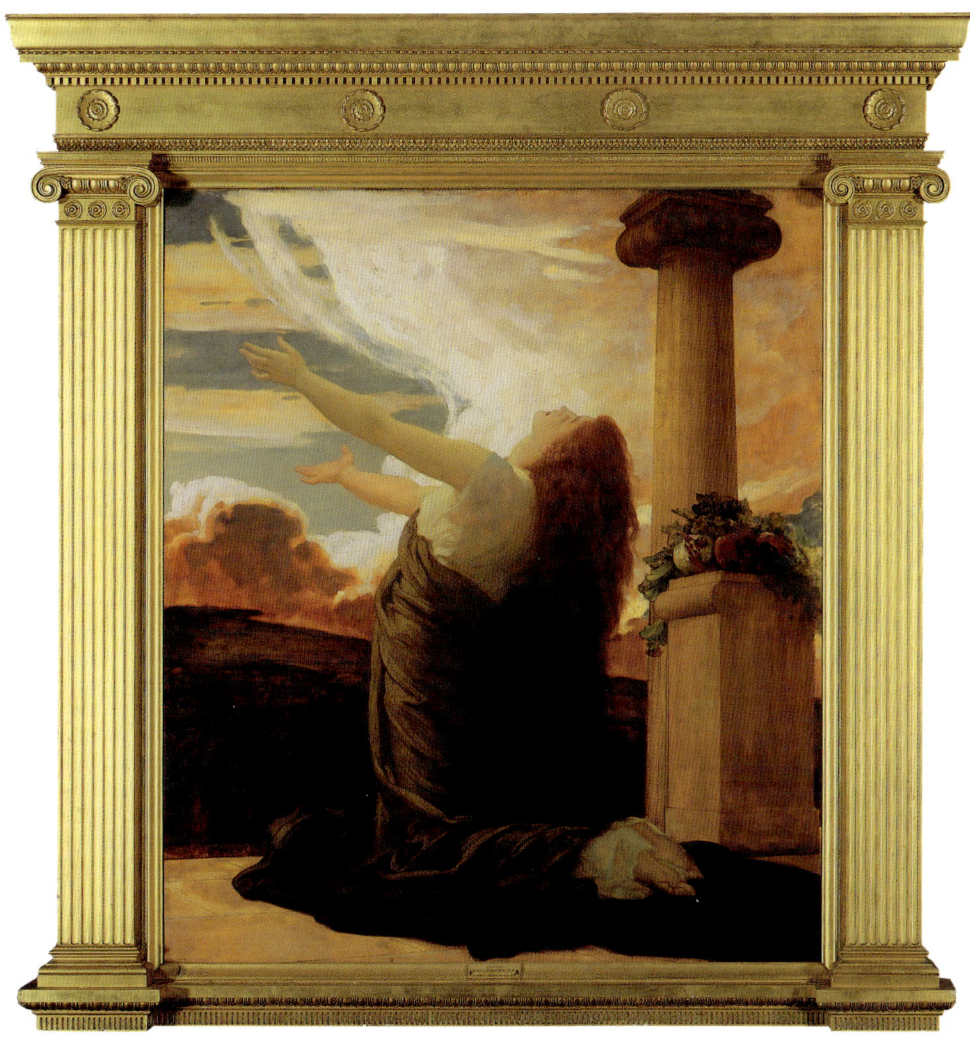

FREDERIC, LORD LEIGHTON
*Clytie* c.1895-6
oil on canvas 156 x 137 cm
John and Julie Schaeffer Collection

Leighton's last great masterpiece, the picture was left unfinished in the artist's studio at his death, though in spite of illness he had managed to bring it to a near state of completion. The subject is Clytie who was rejected by Apollo as his lover and who is shown in a state of inconsolable grief, her arms stretched out to sense the warmth of the sunlight, while the life drains from the rest of her body. Since the God Apollo is associated with the arts it has been suggested that this picture, like the Gallery's *Cymon and Iphigenia*, could be read as a symbolic statement concerning the transforming power of art and beauty.

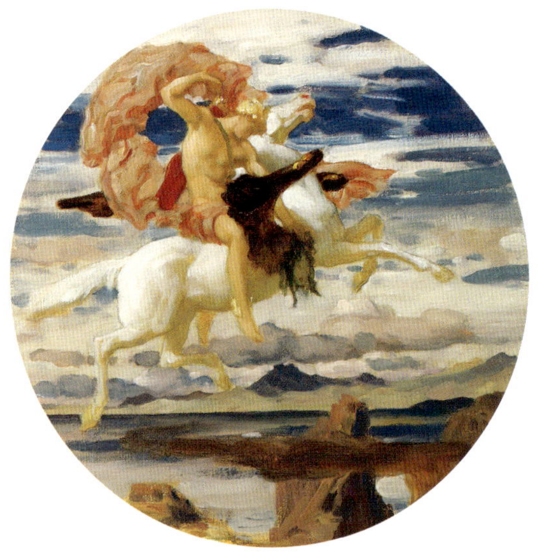

FREDERIC, LORD LEIGHTON
*Perseus on Pegasus hastening to the Rescue of Andromeda* c.1895
oil on canvas 30 x 30 cm
John and Julie Schaeffer Collection

A study for one of Leighton's last works now in the Leicester Art Gallery. The landscape was completed by reference to the sketches the artist had made in Rhodes in 1867 (see p.38). The horse is probably inspired by the Parthenon frieze, a cast from part of which Leighton had in his studio and which he chose to place in the background of his Uffizi *Self-portrait* (see p.37).

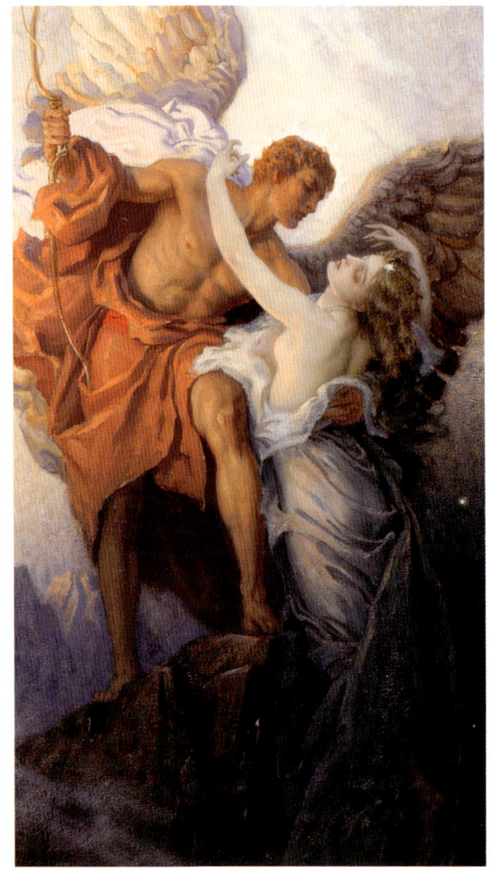

HERBERT JAMES DRAPER (1864-1920)
*Day and the Dawnstar*, c.1906
oil on canvas 54 x 32 cm
John and Julie Schaeffer Collection

Draper was a devoted follower of Leighton and was predicted to become his successor as champion of Classicism. This is a study for a work exhibited by Draper at the Royal Academy in 1906. It shows Apollo, the God of the Sun, reaching out to kiss the lips of the frail Dawnstar, who at that moment, overwhelmed by his radiance, expires. Draper composed a couplet to accompany the picture: 'To faint in the light of the sun she loves/To faint in his light and to die'.

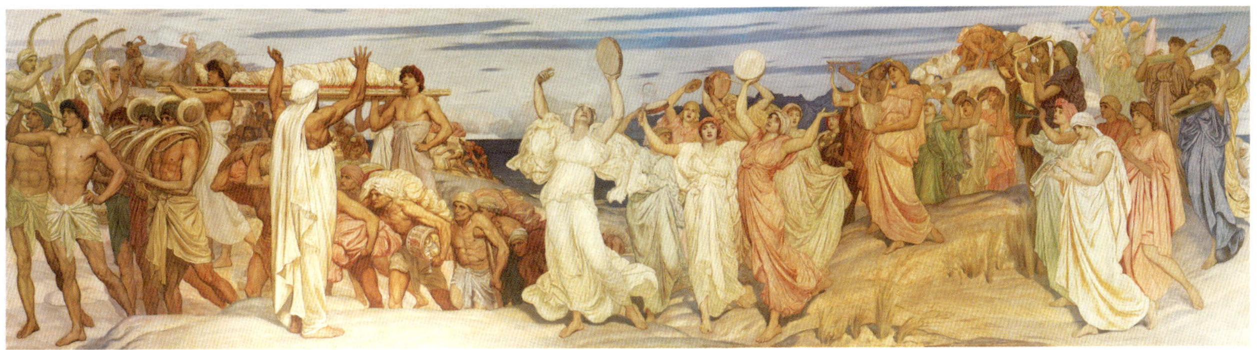

WILLIAM BLAKE RICHMOND (1842-1921)
*The Song of Miriam* 1879-81
oil on canvas 136 x 490 cm
John and Julie Schaeffer Collection

The picture was commissioned in 1879 by William Gilstrap to hang as a pendant to Richmond's earlier *Procession of Bacchus at the Time of the Vintage* of 1869. This had been painted in Rome in emulation of Leighton, the artist even renting the studio in which *Cimabue's Madonna* had been painted. Richmond's two large canvases were to form the principal decoration of the hall of Gilstrap's house, Fornham Park, near Bury St Edmunds. The subject of this canvas is taken from the Book of Exodus and occurs shortly after the Israelites' crossing of the Red Sea: 'And Miriam the prophetess, the sister of Aaron, took a timbrel in her hand, and all the women went out after her with timbrels and with dances'.

# ALMA-TADEMA AND POYNTER

......

Alma-Tadema was Dutch by birth and trained at the Academy of Fine Arts in Antwerp of which he was elected a member in 1861. He began by painting mainly medieval subjects, but a trip to Italy in 1863 inspired him to embark on the detailed reconstructions of the ancient world on which his reputation was built. A work such as the *Juggler* is remarkable for the sense of immediacy it brings to a scene from the remote past. This was Alma-Tadema's aim and his achievement, to make the ancients breath the same air as our own. The effect was achieved by a scrupulous attention to detail and a meticulous technique, and it was a sensational success. Alma-Tadema first exhibited at the Royal Academy in 1869 and encouraged by the favourable reception of his works moved to England in the following year. He became an Associate of the Royal Academy in 1876 and a Academician in 1879, the year after Leighton's election as President. The popularity of his works permitted him to live in extravagant style. His house in Regent's Park was elaborately decorated and furnished in the style of a Roman villa and when this property was damaged (by a chance explosion) he bought the house in Saint John's Wood which had formerly belonged to the painter James Tissot and again fitted it out as a Roman palace.

Poynter pursued his artistic education in Rome, where he became friends with Leighton (six years his senior), and in Paris where he was a fellow student with Whistler in the studio of Charles Gleyre. He returned to England in 1860 and set about painting archaeological reconstructions of the ancient world sometimes on a vastly ambitious scale. In 1868 he became an Associate of the Royal Academy and in 1876 he was elected an Academician. Much of Poynter's career was taken up with teaching and administrative duties. Until 1881 he was Slade Professor of Fine Art at University College, London, and Director of Art and Principal of the National Art Training School at South Kensington. In 1894 he became Director of the National Gallery and in 1896 President of the Royal Academy. During the 1880s he had a period of fewer official duties which enabled him to spend more time on his own painting. The most ambitious of his later works, the *Visit of the Queen of Sheba to King Solomon*, was painted over a period of six years at this time.

Whilst Leighton's Classicism was predominantly concerned with creating an aesthetic ideal, Alma-Tadema's and Poynter's work stressed archaeological accuracy. Both artists sought to represent events of the ancient world as they might in reality have appeared. Yet whereas Poynter's interests lay in the portrayal of the noble personages and events of antiquity, Alma-Tadema's was directed increasingly toward casual incidents from the everyday life of the ancients. To these he brought an anecdotal and sentimental quality which struck a deep chord of sympathy with his Victorian audience. In Alma-Tadema's later work there is also often an underlying mood of chaste eroticism. It was essentially this quality which was developed in the work of one of his principal followers, John William Godward, who specialised in the depiction of sensuous female beauty in an antique setting of clear skies and polished marble.

• **Sir Edward John Poynter** *The Visit of the Queen of Sheba to King Solomon* 1884-1890 (detail)

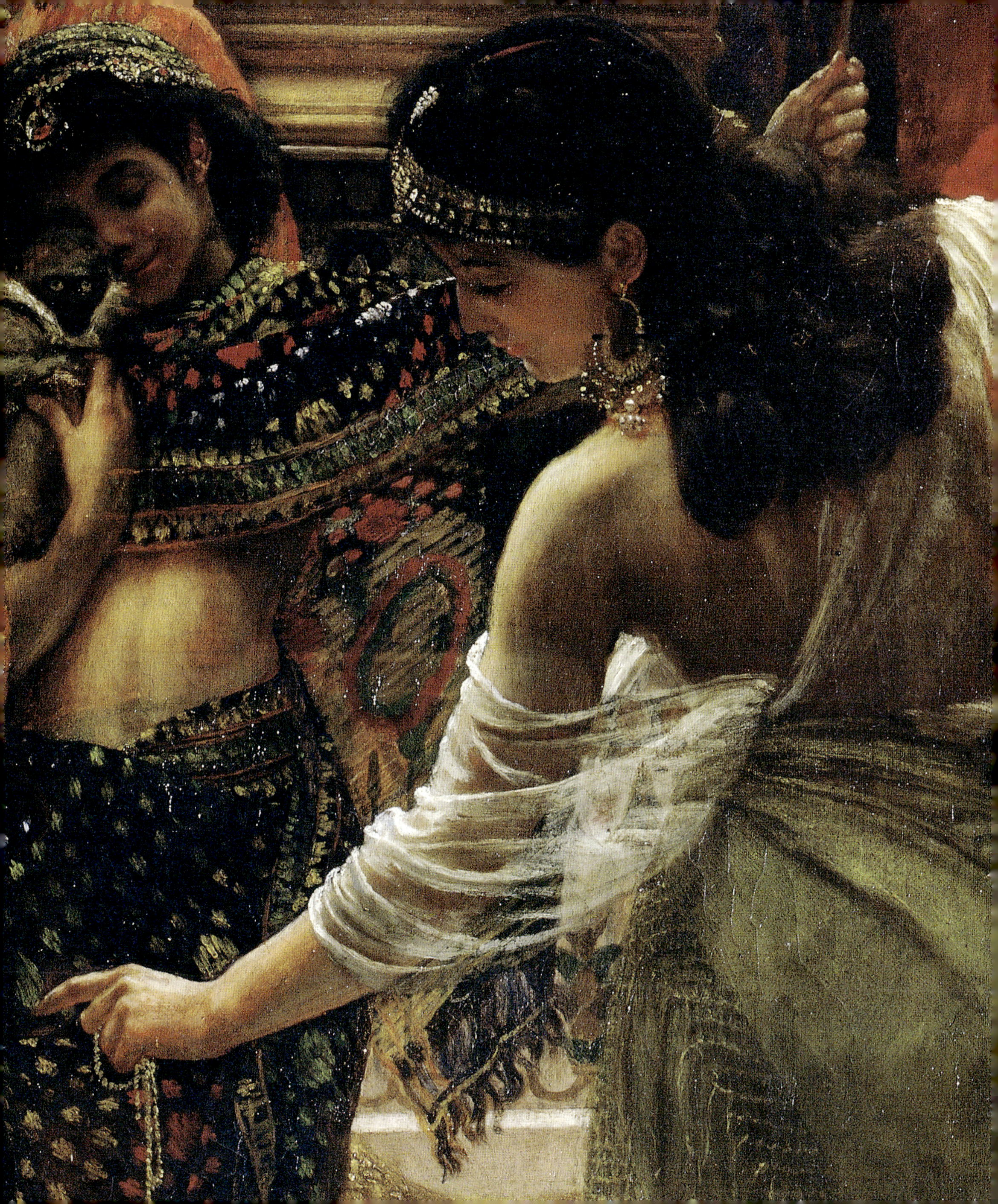

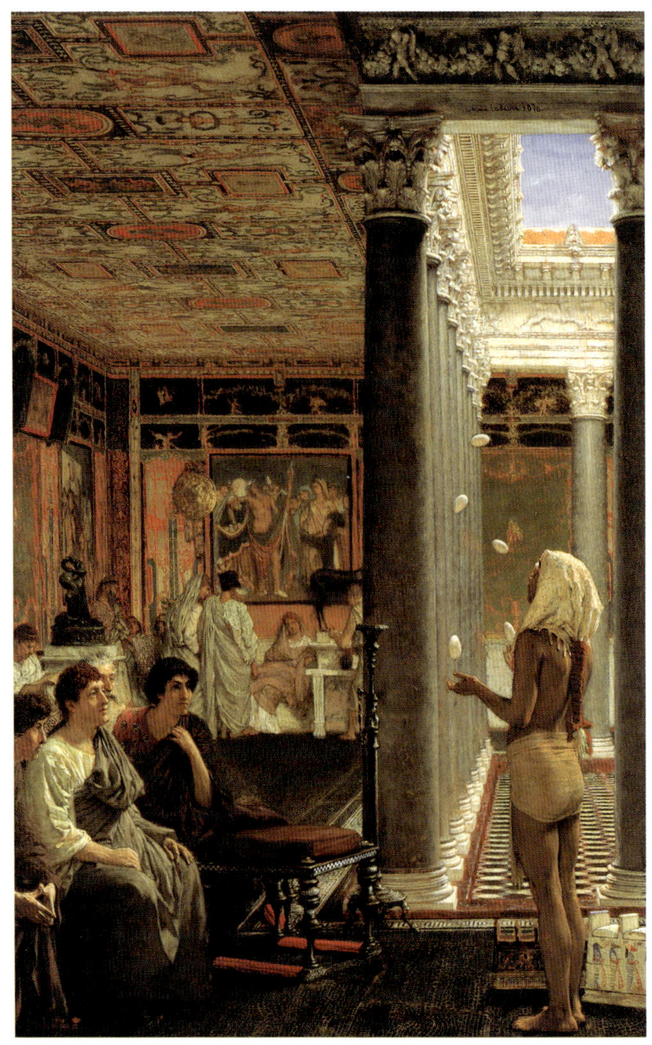

SIR LAWRENCE ALMA-TADEMA (1836-1912)
*A Juggler* 1870
oil on panel 78.7 x 50.1 cm
Art Gallery of New South Wales, gift of John and Julie Schaeffer 1999

An Egyptian egg-juggler entertains a leisured group of patricians in an opulent Pompeian villa. Painted shortly after Alma-Tadema's arrival in London, the subject combines the artist's interests in ancient Egypt and Imperial Rome. As with most of Alma-Tadema's works, many of the props used are authentic pieces. Thus the bronze statues are copied from specific examples, as is the fresco on the back wall. The artist assembled an extensive collection of archaeological drawings, photographs and reference books which permitted him to achieve unprecedented levels of historical accuracy.

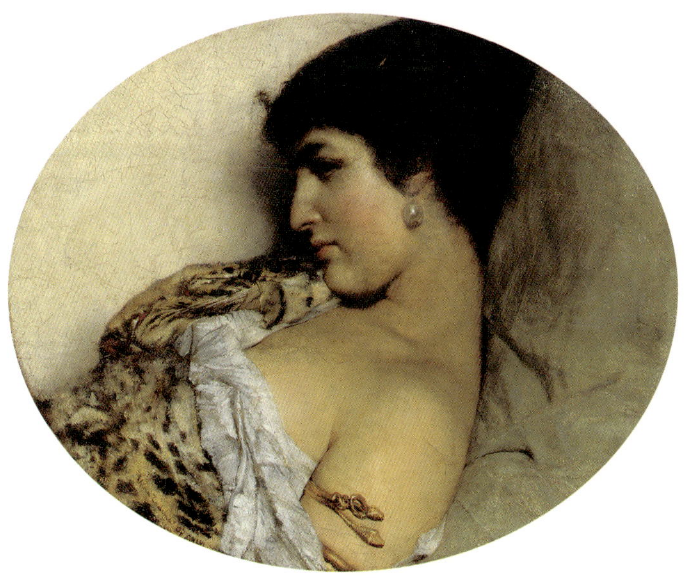

SIR LAWRENCE ALMA-TADEMA
*Cleopatra* 1875
oil on canvas mounted on board 54.6 x 66.7 cm
Art Gallery of New South Wales, gift of Sir Herbert Thompson 1920

Like many nineteenth-century painters Alma-Tadema was attracted to the subject of Cleopatra, who was seen as the epitome of the *femme fatale*. The present work was exhibited at the Royal Academy in 1876, and a second version was painted in the following year (now Auckland Art Gallery). In 1883 the artist produced a full-scale picture of *The Meeting of Anthony and Cleopatra*. In this work he focuses on the dark beauty and fleshly allure of the last Queen of Egypt.

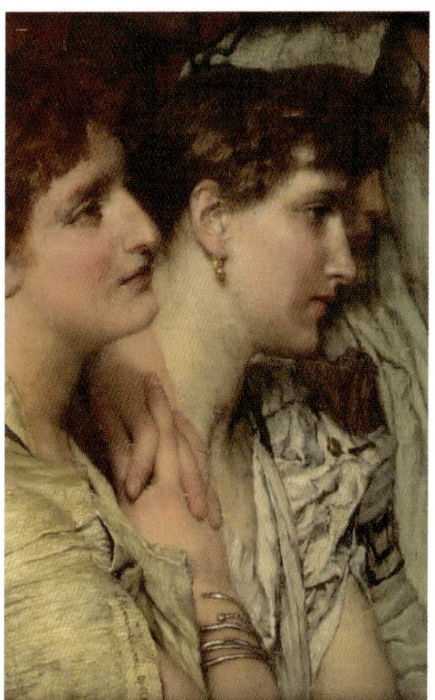

SIR LAWRENCE ALMA-TADEMA
*An Audience*, 1881/2
oil on panel 24 x 15 cm
John and Julie Schaeffer Collection

This curious work was given by Alma-Tadema to the artist George Henry Boughton in 1881. It was then reworked in the following year for the major exhibition of Alma-Tadema's work held at the Grosvenor Gallery. It was there seen and admired by the critic F.G. Stephens who described it as 'remarkable for the variety and characteristic earnestness of the expressions, and for the solidity, delicacy, and brilliancy of the carnations'.

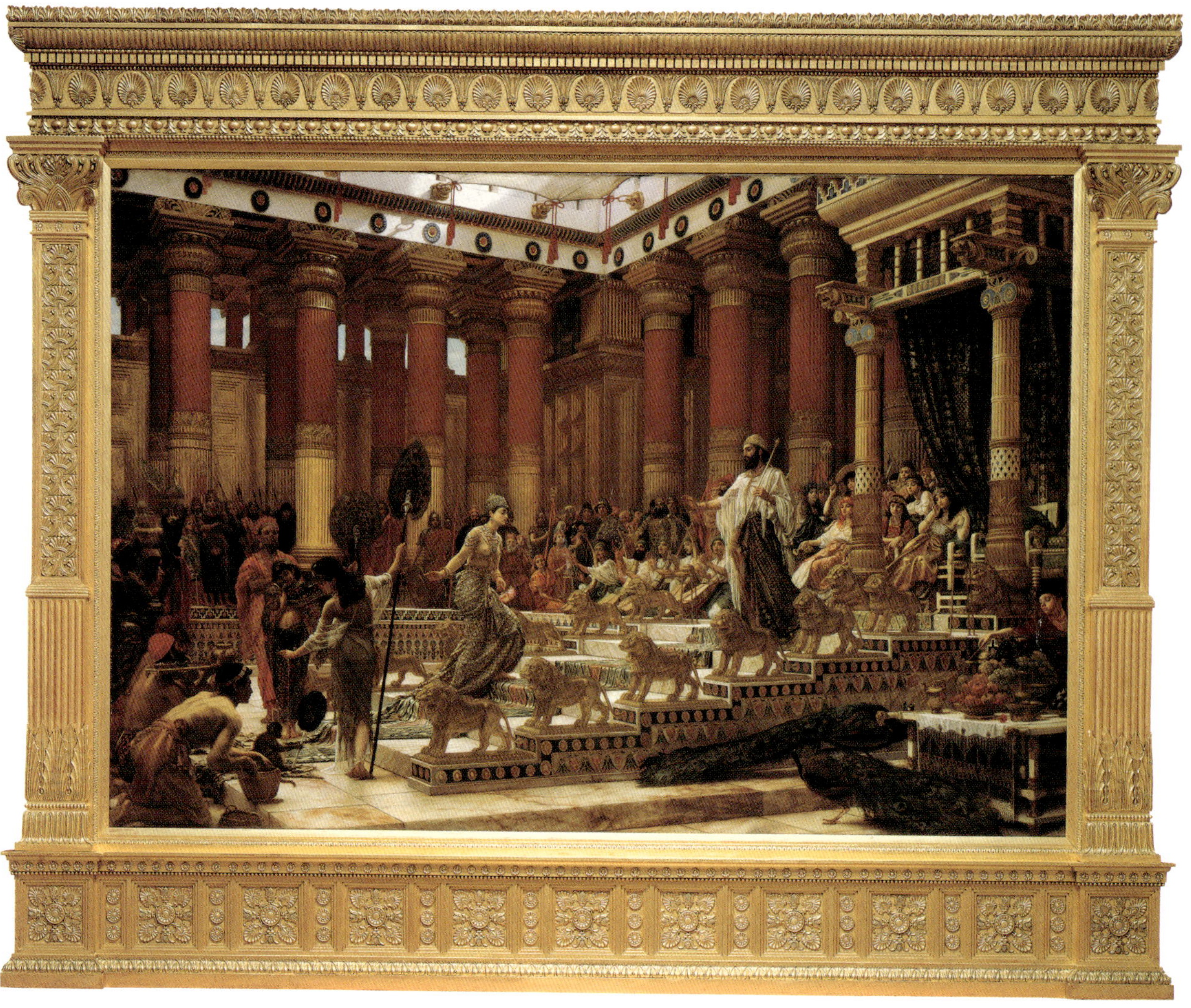

SIR EDWARD JOHN POYNTER (1836-1919)
*The Visit of the Queen of Sheba to King Solomon* 1883-90
oil on canvas 234.5 x 350.4 cm
Art Gallery of New South Wales, purchased 1892

The subject is taken from the Book of Kings: 'When the Queen of Sheba heard of the fame of Solomon … she came to test him with hard questions', but she found herself overwhelmed by his wisdom and glory. 'All the wisdom of Solomon', the Bible recounts, 'the house that he had built, the food of his table, the seating of his officials and the attendance of his servants, their clothing, his cupbearers, and his burnt offerings … [ensured] there was no more spirit in her'. The painting was begun in 1883, but Poynter's painstaking working methods and concern for archaeological accuracy resulted in its taking six years to complete the work.

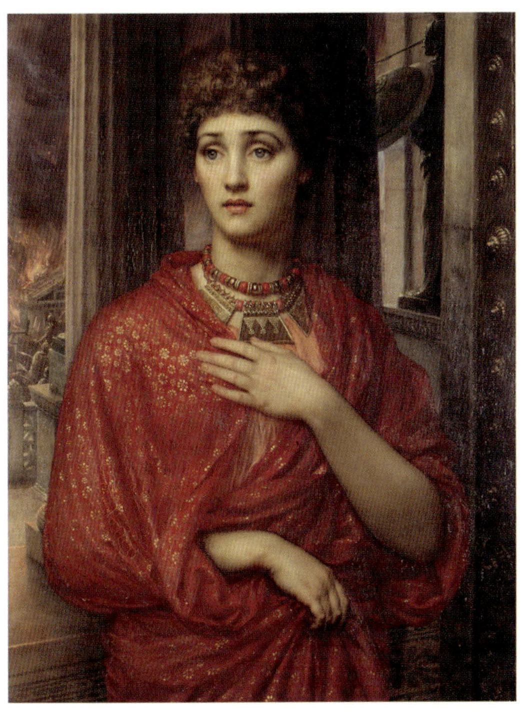

SIR EDWARD JOHN POYNTER
*Helen* 1881
oil on canvas 91.7 x 71.5 cm
Art Gallery of New South Wales, purchased 1968

Helen of Troy was the wife of Menelaus and reputed for her great beauty. Her abduction by Paris precipitated the Trojan War. When this painting was exhibited at the Royal Academy in 1881 the catalogue included a verse, possibly written by William Morris, which describes Helen: 'As in a trance, her eyes look forth afar, / All passionless, with something of amaze / Wondering, perchance, that men should madly mar / With furious strife their own and others' days'.

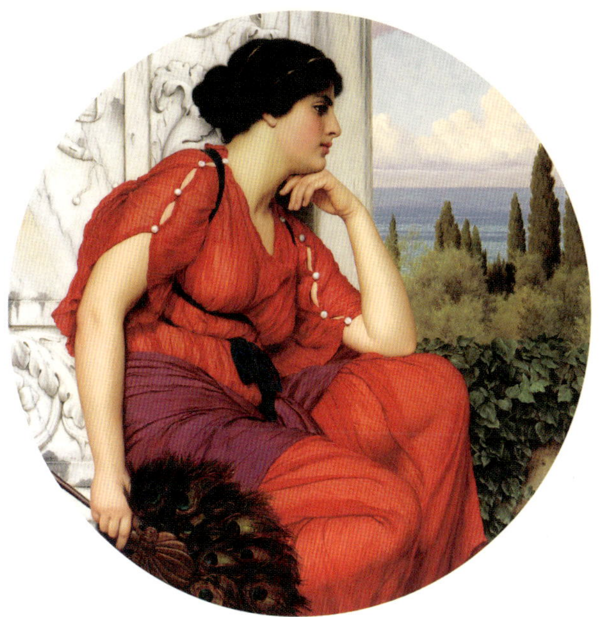

JOHN WILLIAM GODWARD (1861-1922)
*Reverie* 1910
oil on canvas 100.4 x 100.4 cm
John and Julie Schaeffer Collection

This is a characteristic example of Godward's personal variation on the style and subject matter of Alma-Tadema. It combines colouristic intensity with a strictly classical relief composition, the *tondo* format also suggesting High Renaissance prototypes. The woman is holding a fan or sunshade of peacock feathers.

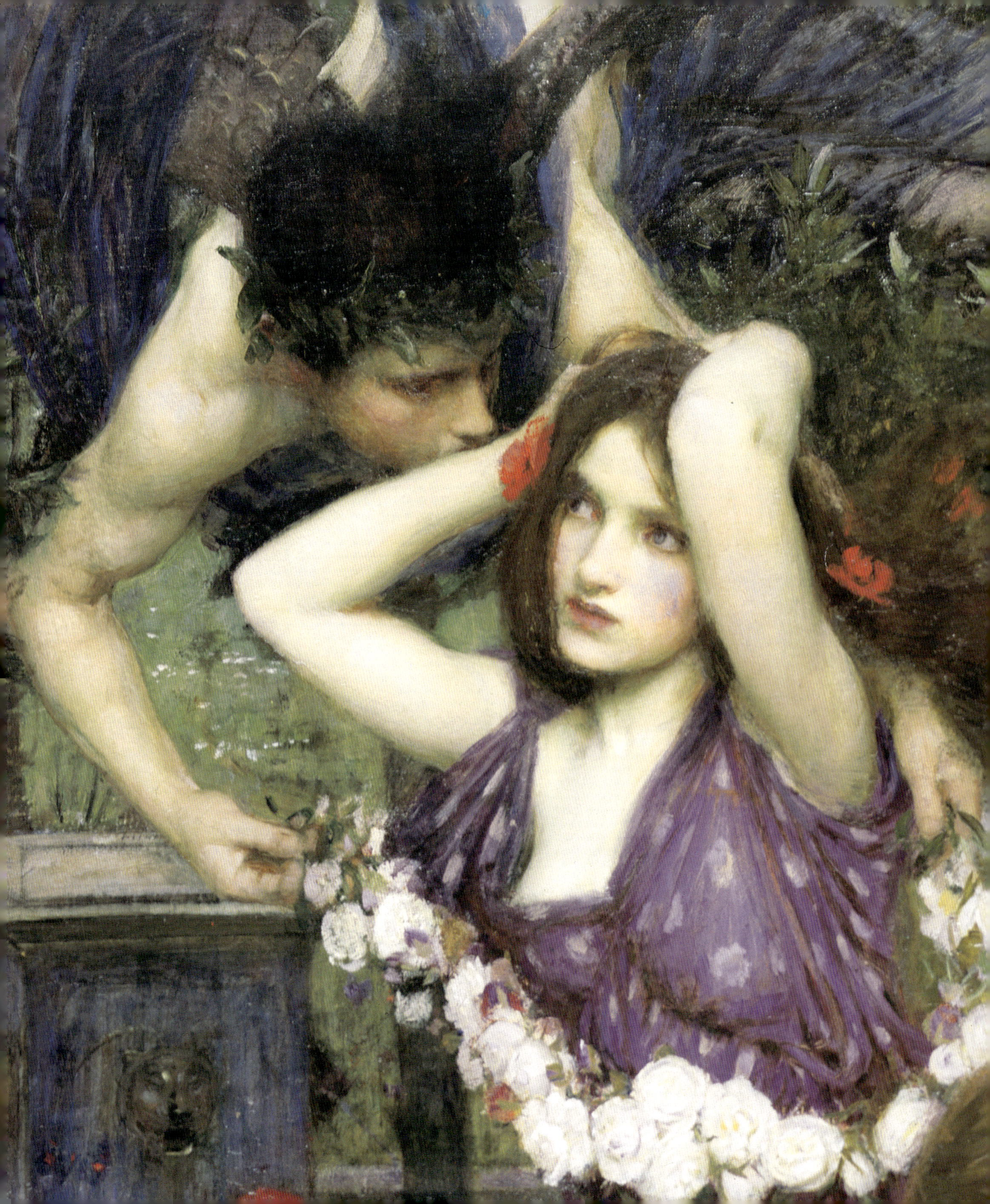

# WATERHOUSE

......

Among the last heirs to Pre-Raphaelitism was an artist who has enjoyed a significant revival of interest in recent years, John William Waterhouse (1849-1917). He was born in Rome where both his mother and father were working as painters and began his training in his father's studio before entering the Royal Academy Schools in 1870. He first exhibited at the Royal Academy in 1874, his early work being strongly influenced by Alma-Tadema, though he painted on a larger scale and in a broader technique.

The *Diogenes* of 1882 is an example of the antique subjects with which Waterhouse achieved a considerable success in the 1880s. However his Royal Academy exhibit of 1888 marked a new departure. This was his most famous painting, *The Lady of Shallott* (Tate Gallery), which represents a return to the medieval romanticism of the Pre-Raphaelites and Burne-Jones. Such subject matter is combined in Waterhouse's case, however, with a more modern technique which reflects the influence of French plein-air naturalism, transmitted in all probability through the works of the painters of the Newlyn School.

Waterhouse was elected an Associate of the Royal Academy in 1885 and a full Academician in 1895. He exhibited a succession of large-scale multi-figured compositions drawing his subject matter from the poetry of Keats and Tennyson, for example, from Shakespeare, from Boccaccio, or from Greek mythology. In contrast to the decorative linear style of Burne-Jones and his followers, Waterhouse's works are decidedly painterly. He invests the old Pre-Raphaelite subjects with a new kind of realism based not on meticulous observation of detail, but on an ability to convey a convincing sense both of atmosphere and psychological tension.

• **John William Waterhouse** *Flora and the Zephyrs* 1897 (detail)

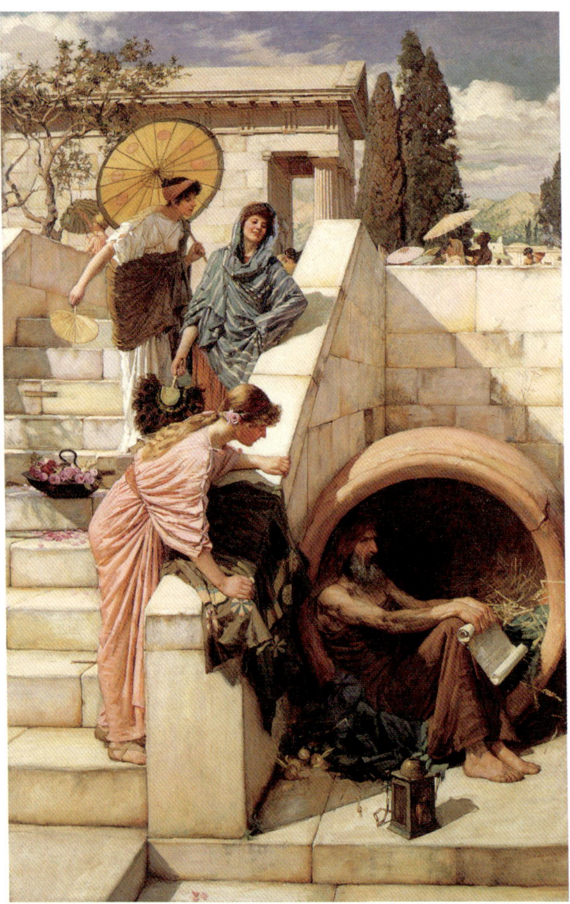

JOHN WILLIAM WATERHOUSE (1849-1917)
*Diogenes* 1882
oil on canvas 208.3 x 134.6 cm
Art Gallery of New South Wales, purchased 1886

Waterhouse's early success of the 1880s was based on classical subjects such as this which show a strong debt to the art of Alma-Tadema. The most famous of the Cynic philosophers, Diogenes (412?-323 BCE) was a colourful and eccentric figure who pursued to an extreme degree the Cynic ideal of a natural life independent of the non-essential luxuries of civilization. He made his life an example of this principle by living in a large 'tub' (i.e. a jar) rather than a house. Reputedly he went about Athens holding a lantern in the daytime claiming to be searching out an honest man, but never to have found one.

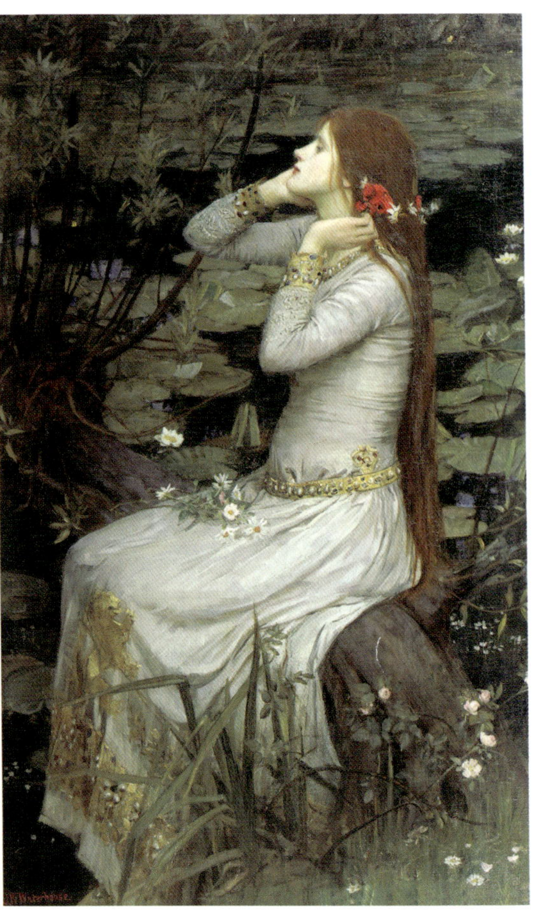

JOHN WILLIAM WATERHOUSE
*Ophelia* 1894
oil on canvas 124.4 x 73.6 cm
John and Julie Schaeffer Collection

From 1888 many of Waterhouse's themes were drawn from the repertoire of the Pre-Raphaelites. The subject of *Ophelia* had been treated most famously, of course, by Millais in 1852 (Tate Gallery). Waterhouse painted the subject on three occasions, first in 1889, the present picture in 1894 and a final version in 1910. He chose in this instance to represent the moment immediately preceding Ophelia's death when in her madness she came to 'a willow grows aslant a brook … with fantastic garlands … Of crow-flowers, nettles, daisies and long purples …'.

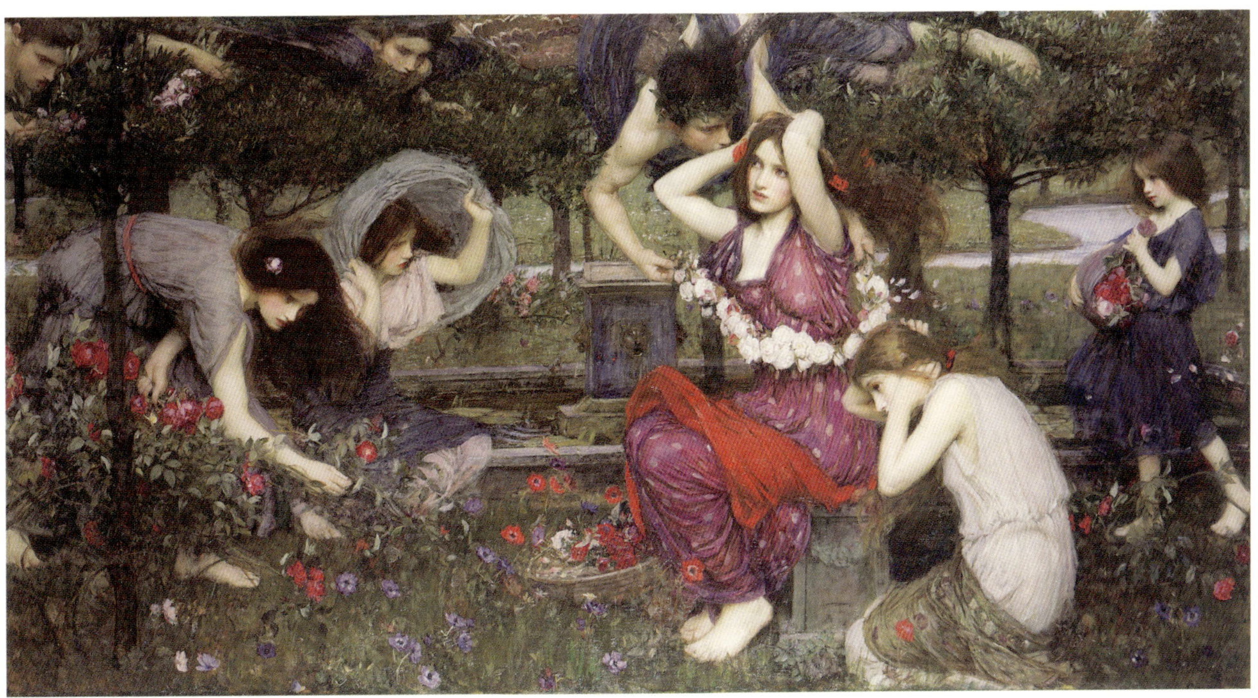

JOHN WILLIAM WATERHOUSE
*Flora and the Zephyrs* 1897
oil on canvas 111 x 206 cm
John and Julie Schaeffer Collection

The subject is here taken from Ovid's *Fasti*. The nymph Flora was abducted by the wind-god Zephyr who took her as his bride and gave her a fruitful garden saying 'Goddess be queen of flowers'. Waterhouse shows Flora gathering flowers with her companions at the moment when Zephyr in the trees has just caught sight of her and fallen in love with her. He places his lips to her arm and captures her in a garland of roses. The picture is one of Waterhouse's most important and characteristic works. It was exhibited at the Royal Academy in 1898 to considerable acclaim.

# LEIGHTON AND THE 'NEW SCULPTURE'

......

The last two decades of the nineteenth century witnessed a remarkable renaissance in the art of sculpture in Britain. It would be difficult to overestimate the importance of Leighton's part in bringing this about. It was the radical new naturalism and energy of his *Athlete strangling a Python* exhibited at the Royal Academy in 1877 which is generally seen as marking the breakthrough. It was not, however, Leighton himself who saw through the revolution. He made only two more finished statues, the life-size *Sluggard* and the small-scale *Needless Alarms* both exhibited in 1886. His influence was felt, besides the example he set in the *Athlete*, in the encouragement he gave to a younger generation of sculptors.

It has often been remarked that Leighton's paintings are highly sculptural in feeling. His style of drapery painting was heavily dependent on his study of antique statuary. And his thinking in sculptural terms seems to have been reflected in his teaching at the Royal Academy life school. Among the young sculptors who benefited from his support and encouragement were Thomas Brock, Hamo Thornycroft and Albert Gilbert.

With Brock there was a professional association since it was to the younger sculptor that Leighton turned when it came to enlarging his ideas for the *Athlete* to life-size proportions and casting the figure in bronze. Thornycroft was to become a close friend and admiring disciple of Leighton and in his journal recorded with deep affection the encouragement which the older artist gave to himself and his fellows. It must have been greatly to his satisfaction that a copy of the bronze reduction of *Teucer* was acquired by Leighton and displayed in his studio.

The most important of the young sculptors in the 'New Sculpture' movement was Alfred Gilbert. He was at once the most talented, the most original and the most ambitious sculptor of the late Victorian era. He trained in London with the Hungarian-born sculptor Joseph Edgar Boehm and at the Ecole des Beaux-Arts in Paris where he absorbed the fashionable Beaux-Arts taste for the heroic nude. During six years spent in Italy he studied the work of Donatello and Cellini which inspired his interest in the medium of bronze. In 1882 he sent his *Perseus arming* to the Grosvenor Gallery where Leighton admired it and determined on his next visit to Italy to seek out its author. At this time he himself commissioned from Gilbert a bronze statuette on a subject which he left to the artist's choice, a commission which resulted in the *Icarus* of 1884.

On his return to London Gilbert received a succession of major commissions of which the most conspicuous were the Jubilee Monument to Queen Victoria, the Shaftesbury Memorial in Piccadilly Circus, London (for which he invented the famous figure of *Eros*, symbolic of the philanthropic Lord Shaftesbury's love for humanity) and the tomb of the Duke of Clarence at Windsor. Sadly his slow working methods and disregard for financial affairs led to his bankruptcy in 1901 and a self-imposed exile of 25 years in Belgium. Only in 1926 did he return to London to execute his last major commission, the memorial to Queen Alexandria at Marlborough Gate, London. He received a knighthood on its completion in 1932.

• **Sir Alfred Gilbert** *Perseus arming* (detail)

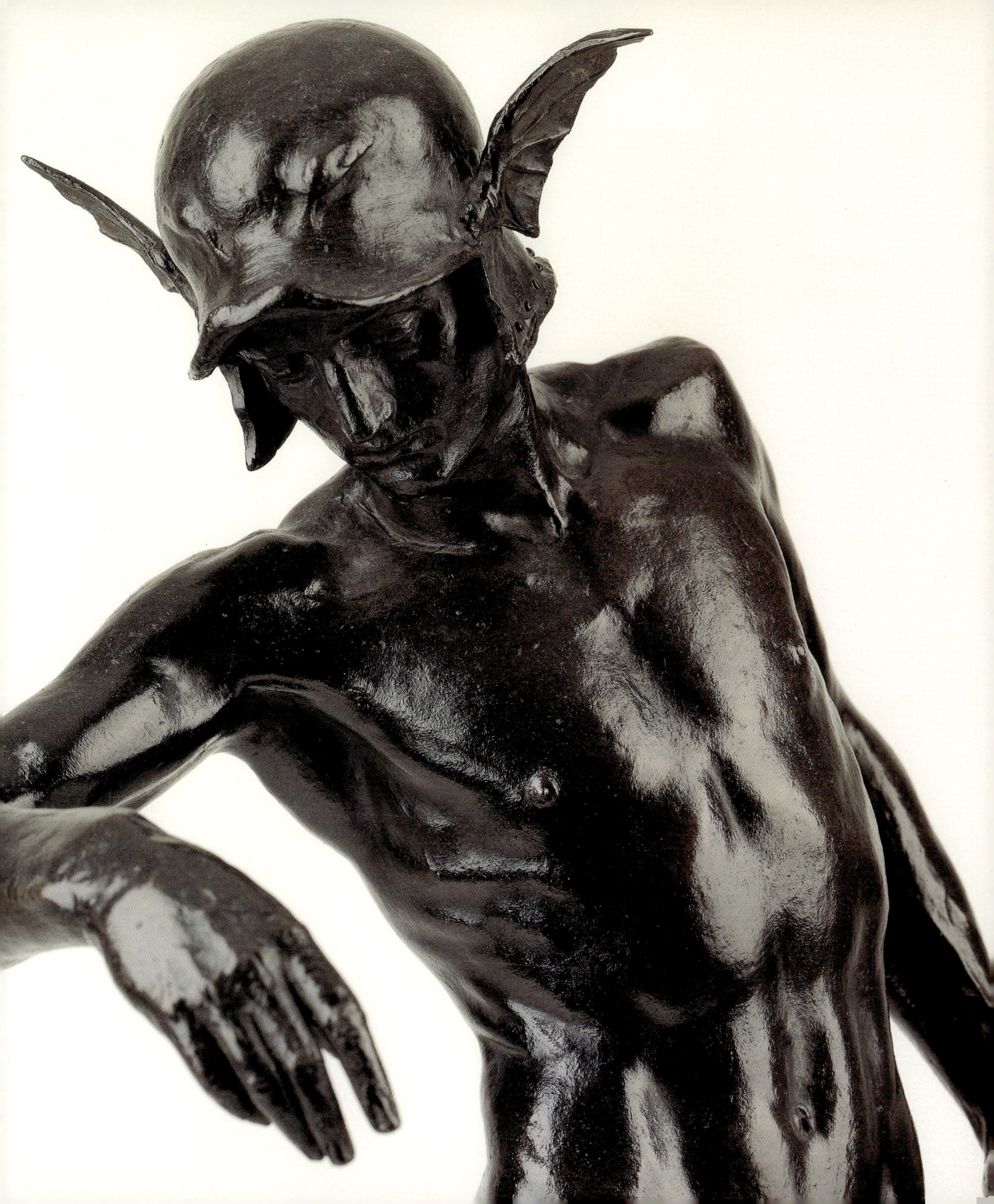

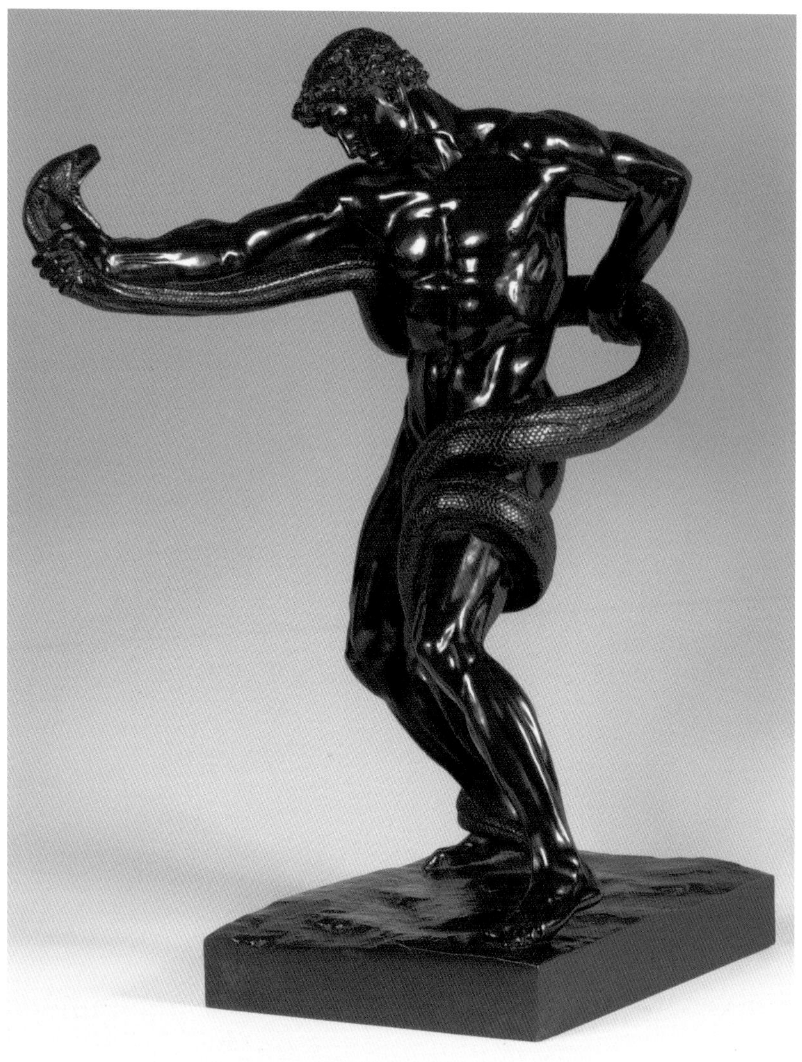

FREDERIC, LORD LEIGHTON (1830-1896)
*Athlete strangling a Python*
the original 1874-7
bronze, height 52 cm
John and Julie Schaeffer collection

Leighton began work on his first major work of sculpture in 1874 having little experience beyond the small plaster models which he sometimes made in preparing his paintings. To enlarge the figure to life-size and to cast it in bronze he sought the assistance of Thomas Brock who dealt with the mechanics of the procedure without interfering with the artistic integrity of the conception. When the completed life-size bronze was exhibited at the Royal Academy in 1877 it was immediately recognised as something quite new. The flaccid conventions of neoclassical idealism had been replaced by a torsion which depended on a detailed observation of anatomical detail.

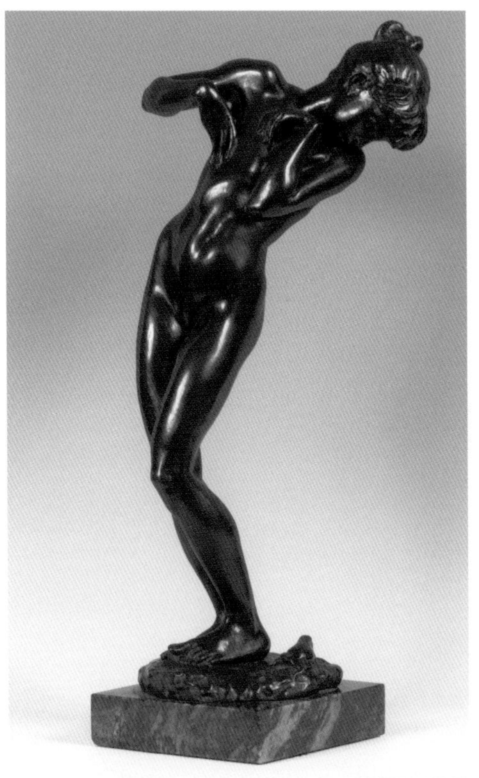

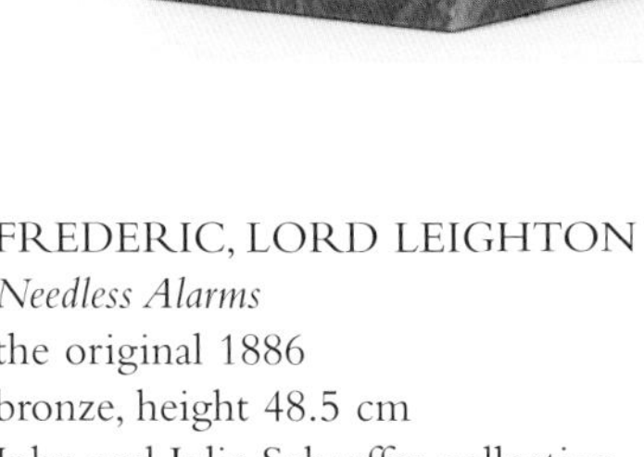

FREDERIC, LORD LEIGHTON
*Needless Alarms*
the original 1886
bronze, height 48.5 cm
John and Julie Schaeffer collection

The original was exhibited along with *The Sluggard* at the Royal Academy in 1886, but as a statuette rather than a life-size figure. Leighton was involved in producing reduced bronze editions of his only two major works of sculpture, but this work was conceived in the first place on a small scale and, not without humour, as a decorative object. The sensuality of the medium is diffused by an anecdotal quality which is rare in Leighton's work.

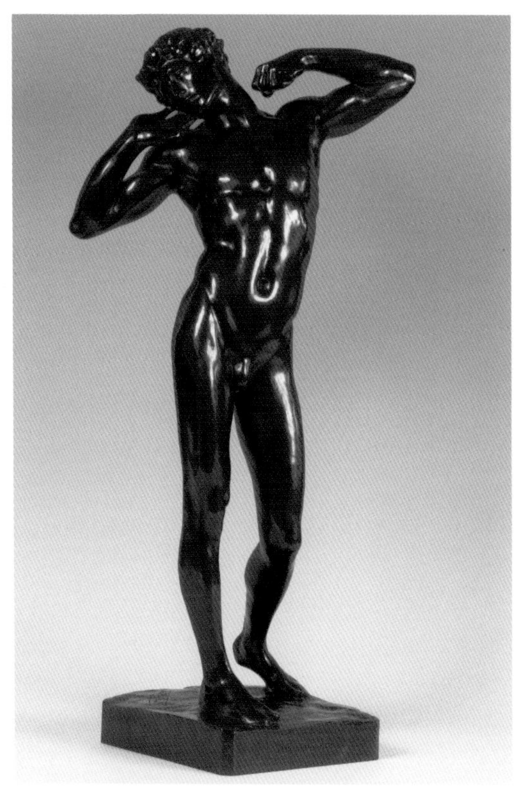

FREDERIC, LORD LEIGHTON
*The Sluggard*
the original 1885
bronze, height 51.5 cm
John and Julie Schaeffer collection

The pose was reputedly inspired by the sight of one of Leighton's Italian life models, Giuseppe Valone, stretching languorously after a sitting. It probably owes much also to the example of Gilbert's *Perseus arming* which Leighton had admired at the Grosvenor Gallery in 1882. The life-size bronze was exhibited at the Royal Academy in 1886 with the title *An Athlete awakening from Sleep* and it has sometimes been regarded as a pendant to the earlier *Athlete strangling a Python*. The figure is related to a number which appear in Leighton paintings, but in bronze attains a sensuality which the artist either avoided, or which eluded him, in paint.

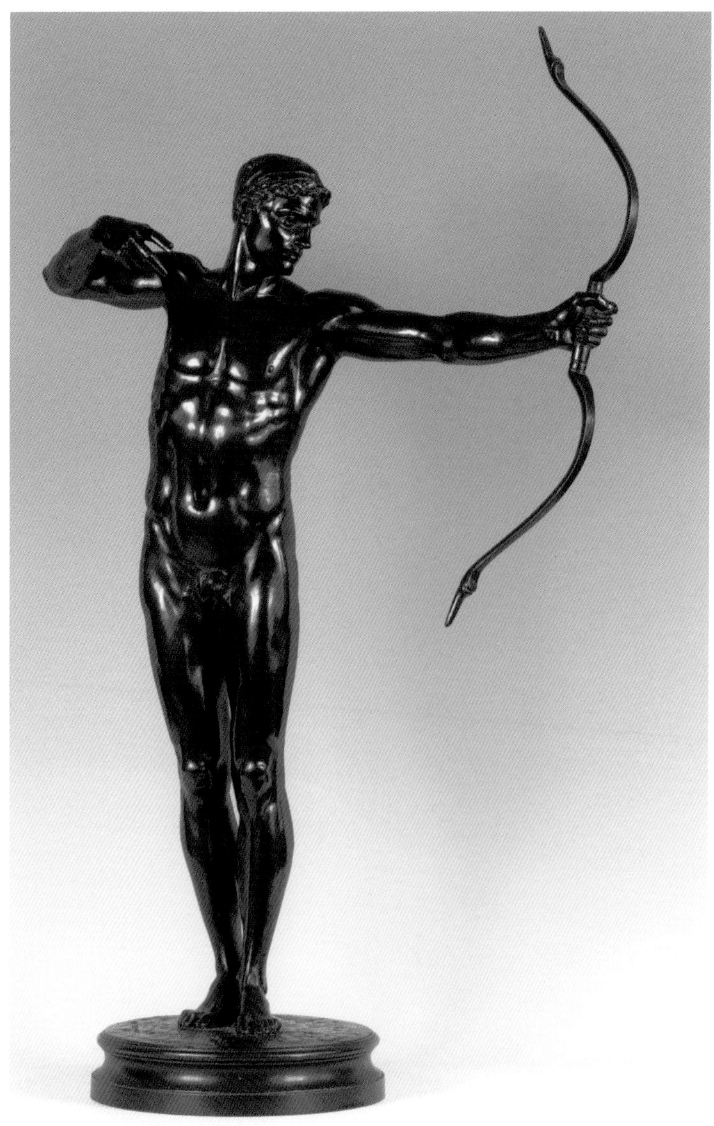

SIR WILLIAM HAMO THORNYCROFT (1850-1925)
*Teucer*
the original plaster 1881, this cast 1904
bronze, height 74 cm
John and Julie Schaeffer Collection

Thornycroft was a close friend of Leighton and received much encouragement from him in his career as a sculptor. He exhibited the full-size plaster of *Teucer* at the Royal Academy in 1881, with a quotation in the catalogue from Pope's translation of the Iliad describing Teucer's attempts to kill Hector. A full-scale bronze was exhibited at the RA in the following year (Tate Gallery). It was admired for its boldly orthogonal composition and the detailed naturalism of the musculature. This is one of the reduced versions with Thornycroft produced subsequently, one of which was acquired by Leighton and displayed in his studio.

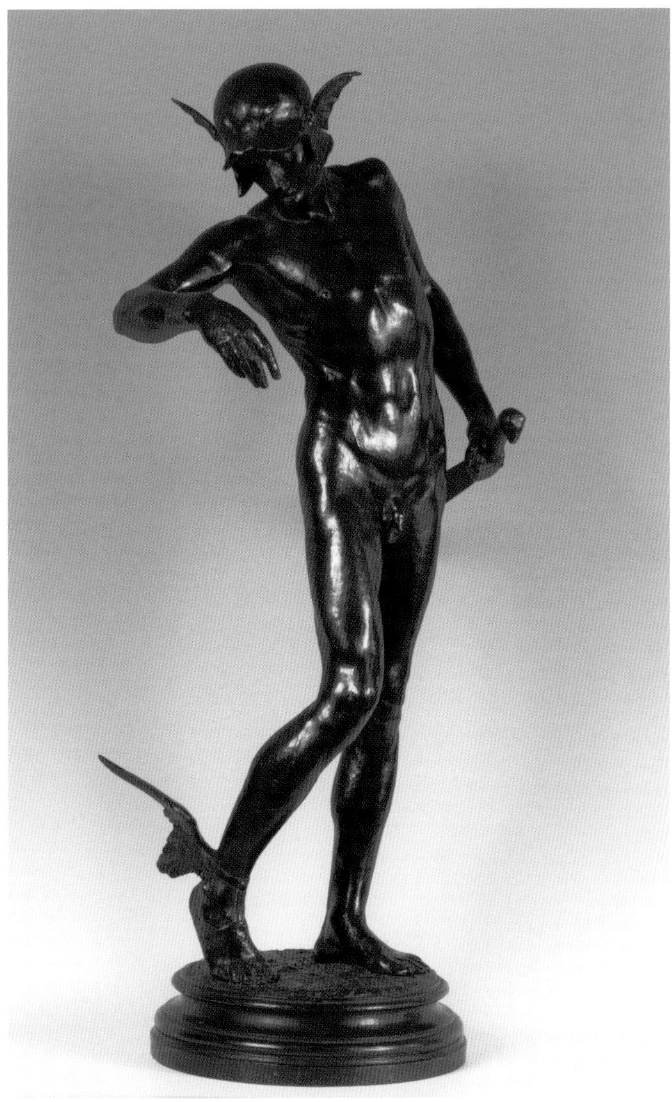

SIR ALFRED GILBERT (1854-1934)
*Perseus arming*
the original 1882
bronze, height 70 cm
John and Julie Schaeffer Collection

The figure was inspired by Cellini's *Perseus with the Head of Medusa* in Loggia dei Lanzi, Florence, a famous example of bronze casting by the lost-wax method, a process which Gilbert was largely responsible for reviving in the nineteenth century. The Schaeffer example is an especially crisp and vibrant casting which shows the full extent of Gilbert's mastery of the sensual possibilities of the medium. Perseus is shown arming himself with the winged sandals loaned to him by the God Mercury for his encounter with the Gorgon Medusa. As in the case of the following two pieces, the idea had autobiographical significance for Gilbert who was at the time 'arming himself' with the skills necessary to pursue an outstanding career.

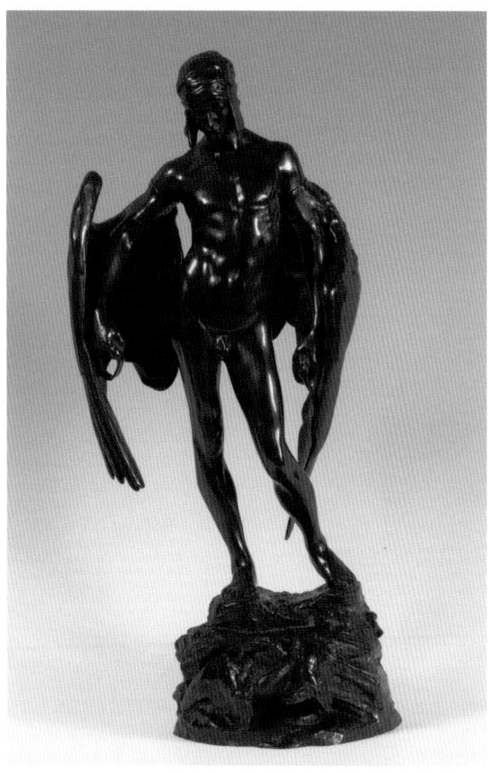

SIR ALFRED GILBERT
*Icarus*
the original 1884
bronze, height 49.5 cm
John and Julie Schaeffer Collection

This is a later reduction of the statuette commissioned by Leighton and exhibited to acclaim at the Royal Academy in 1884. Leighton left the choice of subject and treatment to the artist. Gilbert opted for this essay in the manner of Donatello choosing as his subject another mythological figure whom he regarded as having autobiographical significance. Icarus's desire to fly like a bird on wings sealed with wax represents the sculptors struggle with material limitations and his longing for spiritual freedom.

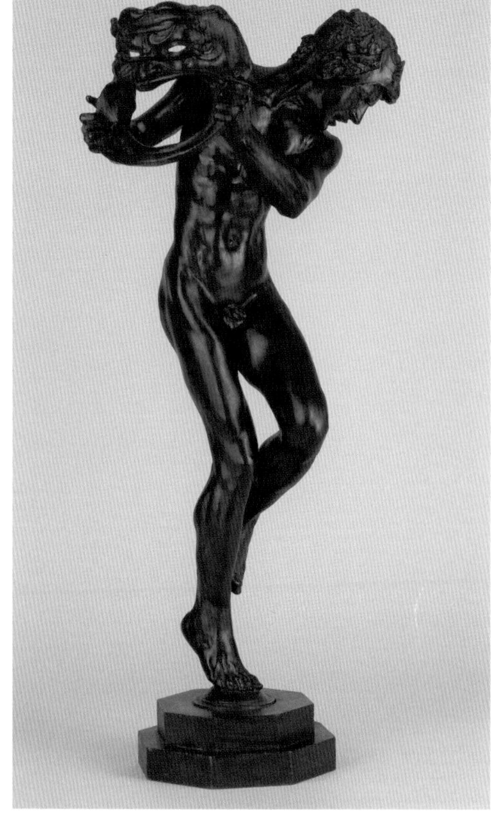

SIR ALFRED GILBERT
*Comedy and Tragedy*
the original plaster 1891-2
bronze, height 73.7 cm
Art Gallery of New South Wales, purchased 1920

This extraordinarily sensuous exercise in Mannerist contrapposto, inspired by Giambologna, is remarkable for the immediacy of the moment is seeks to evoke. A young stage hand is running to deliver a comic mask to the theatre when he is stung by a bee. Gilbert's idea was to convey in a single figure the opposites of Comedy, represented in the mask, and Tragedy as reflected in the expression on the boy's face. The pose at the same time expresses a physical tension between opposing forces. This was the third in Gilbert's trilogy of nude male figures which reflect events in his own life: the mask is that presented in public to conceal increasing difficulties in the artist's personal and professional life.

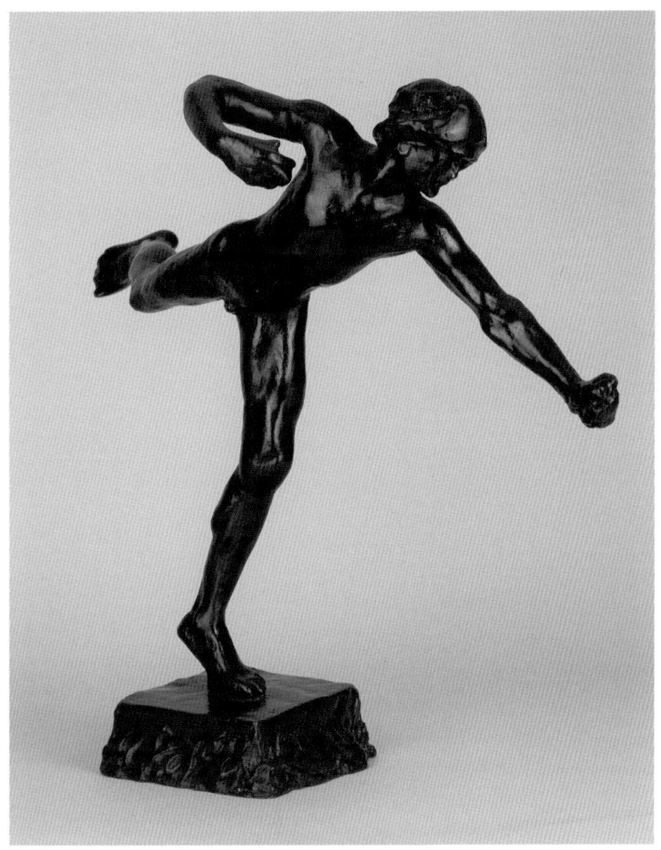

SIR ALFRED GILBERT
*Study for Eros*
the original plaster 1891
bronze, height 61 cm
John and Julie Schaeffer collection

This is a rare bronze version of Gilbert's plaster model for the figure of Eros which crowns his monument to the Earl of Shaftesbury in Piccadilly Circus, London. The original plaster was among those which the artist smashed when he left England in 1901 after his bankruptcy. The pieces were reassembled by the sculptor who took over Gilbert's studio, Henry Hampton, and two bronze casts were then made (now Tate Gallery and Royal Academy). Exceptionally permission was given for a further cast to be made from the Tate bronze as the centre-piece of a memorial to the pupils of Aldenham School – Gilbert's school – who fell in the Second World War, resulting in the present version.

# INDEX OF ARTISTS


**Alma-Tadema**, Sir Lawrence 5, 46, **48-9**, 51, 53-4

**Batten**, John Dickson 21, **26**

**Brown**, Ford Madox 5, 7, **8**

**Burne-Jones**, Sir Edward Coley 21, **22-4**, 25, 27-8, 30, 34

**Burton**, Sir Frederic William **13**

**Draper**, Herbert James **44**

**Fossi**, Paolo **37**

**Frampton**, Edward Reginald 21, **27**

**Frith**, William Powell **11**

**Gilbert**, Sir Alfred 56, 59, **61-3**

**Godward**, John William 46, **51**

**Hunt**, William Holman 7, **10**

**Leighton**, Frederic, Lord 5, 13, 28, 31, 34, **36-44**, 45-6, 56, **58-9**, 60, 62

**Millais**, Sir John Everett 7, **9**, 12-13, 28, 54

**Paton**, Sir Joseph Noel **12**

**Perugini**, Charles Edward **13**

**Poynter**, Sir Edward John 5, 46, **50-1**

**Redgrave**, Richard **11**

**Richmond**, William Blake **45**

**Rossetti**, Dante Gabriel 5, 7, 15, **16-19**, 28, 34

**Stanhope**, John Roddam Spencer 21, **25-6**

**Thornycroft**, Sir William Hamo 56, **60**

**Waterhouse**, John William 5, 53, **54-5**

**Watts**, George Frederic 5, 28, **30-3**